A Heavenly Gift

by
Pauline Johnson

Published by the author
This is edition: 2
Copyright © Pauline Johnson 2020
Pauline Johnson asserts the moral right to
be identified as the sole author of this work.
A catalogue record for this book
is not available from the British Library
Amazon ISBN-9798621296995

Typeset by Montgomery Thompson
Cover by Montgomery Thompson

Names have been changed to protect the privacy of individuals.

Printed and bound by CreateSpace
All Rights Reserved. No part of this publication may be reproduced,
stored in a retrieval system, or transmitted
in any form or by any means, electronic, mechanical, photocopying,
recording or otherwise, without the prior permission of the author.
This book is sold subject to the condition that it shall not,
by way of trade or otherwise, be lent, re-sold, hired out or otherwise
circulated without the author's prior consent
in any form of binding or cover other than which it
is published and without a similar condition including this condition
being imposed on the subsequent publisher.

ACKNOWLEDGEMENTS

I thank God for giving me Serena, my beautiful guardian angel
and for Matt and John my guides.
Without their loving messages, protection, guidance and
patience I would not be doing the work I do.

I have to thank my love Monte for being an amazing partner;
for listening, organising, designing, editing, discussing and
supporting me every step of the way while writing this book.

I also want to thank my family;
my amazing mum, my wonderful dad,
my sister Carmel, and my brothers
Brendan, Noel, Colin, Garry and Nigel.
I have been so blessed to be part of this family.

*Dedicated to my
Angels and Guides.*

Table of Contents

1	Childhood & Children	5
2	Life & Loss	23
3	Senses & Sight	41
4	The Paradox of Perfection	61
5	Saved by Sickness	83
6	Bats & Beginnings	101
7	Levitating Letters	115
8	Livin' in Dyan	127
9	Back to the Beginning	139
10	Eyes & Ears	155
11	Challenges & Courage	171
12	Instincts & Intuition	187
13	Grounded & Growing	203
14	Travelling & Trusting	213
15	Loving & Living	225
16	Walls & Wonders	241
17	Heavenly Lights	257
18	Wandering & Windows	279
19	Heavenly Havens	299
20	Baptism & Birth	315
21	A Heavenly Gift	337
	Conclusion	367

Prologue

The angel appeared before my bed, green light pouring off of him in waves. I was overwhelmed with a powerful sensation of peace and amazement. On his head I could see a white crown, bursting with a dazzling light. Wisps of energy fanned away from him like smoke in a breeze though everything in the room remained completely still. The sheer magnitude of the vision shut out all other senses; no smell, no sound…that is, until he spoke.

"I am Archangel Raphael."

His voice was soft but stunningly powerful. The entire room was filled with the glorious green light that emanated from him. I could not see his face clearly, like it was behind a fog. An Archangel! I stared, shocked, looking for wings but there was only light - beautiful, amazing pale green light like the water in an ocean storm. Somehow I just knew that he was there to heal and help me. My hurts, my sorrows, my doubts, all of the things I kept locked away that had been weighing me down I knew now would start to heal.

A Heavenly Gift

This book was written to share with you the beautiful fact that you are not alone. You matter. You are loved more than you know. You always have been and always will be. I know this because it has been shown to me repeatedly through the messages of love I receive from the angels and the deceased. Many words are used to describe my gifts: psychic, medium, empath, etc., but really, I am all of these things. I write in this book about angels and healing but the experiences have been so much more. What is revealed to me are details of other's lives, sometimes secrets, things they bury within that need healing and light. It is to do with their physical, mental, spiritual and emotional balance. I get to experience their feelings and emotions and see visions of what is going on around them. I have seen demons, the dead, and the angels. People come in desperation sometimes to connect or know more about the people they have lost.

I connect with the dead through God's angels and spirit guides to help heal and give hope. In reality, I just try to get out of the way to let the amazing healing guidance through. I have met with people from every gender and occupation, every social strata and religion. This divine help is available to everyone, every day of their lives if they choose it. I did not choose to do this in my life, in fact it is part of me that took quite a while to embrace. The older I got, the stronger and clearer my gift became. I cannot run away from myself, and I now do not want to run away from the angels and the deceased messages so I have chosen to learn, listen and be still. The guidance comes through guardian angels, given to us by God to bring loving messages of truth and help. I have learned to embrace it, all of it. I love working with the angels and deceased to help other people in all aspects of their lives. This book is filled with readings I have done for others and true experiences of spiritual blessings in my own life.

CHAPTER 1

Childhood & Children

I was born in Chorley, England, in November 1963, the middle child in our family of five boys and two girls. All my siblings were born in Northern Ireland, except me. One of my brothers passed away as a baby, but more about Noel later. We are a very close-knit family, my childhood was happy and I believe what most would consider, normal. Being brought up in a house full of brothers, I was a bit of a tomboy. I could most often be found running through the fields, lying in the rushes and making forts in the hedges when we went to live in the countryside. The thought of angels and the deceased was far from my mind as a child, but the occasional paranormal experience wasn't unusual to me. I would be a lot older before I started to connect to the angels and my guides. The spirits of the deceased are just as real to me now as the living. As adults we can learn a lot from remembering our own childhood. Children look at life through the eyes of innocence. When we need a fresh perspective in our adult lives we should use more of our own childlike energy and trust we are being looked after and call on our angels to help.

The first time I had any sense of the spirit world I was about seven years old. I remember being out on a drive with my parents and the rest of my family. Growing up, my dad had a love of fast motorcars I think I get this trait from him as I also love cars, which in those days being in Northern Ireland wasn't very common. On this particular day the whole family was packed into the car for a drive. It was in the 1970s and no one wore seat belts then so I was standing behind my mother's seat, looking up at an old ruined house on a hill.

A feeling of great sadness came to me and I said to my mother, "There is someone in that house and they are very sad mum."

My mother laughed, "Pauline, no one lives there, it's all falling down."

Many years later as an adult, I was driving with a friend of mine and we passed the same house and started to talk about it. They knew a lot about the history of the place and told me that the person who had lived there died of suicide and no-one had found them for a day or two. Even after so many years I just knew that they still needed prayer. It was my first feeling of the energy of the dead that I can remember as a child, but I would be in my forties before I would realise I had spiritual gifts to connect with the deceased. It was being older and much later in my life, and near that same old ruin of that house I got to see my first fully formed spirit of a person.

Growing up, my father and mother were bar owners. We owned bars first in Belfast, then Downpatrick, Stewartstown, and finally Coleraine (all of these places are based in Northern Ireland). As a child I didn't speak much and I liked to wear my hair very long so it covered my face. I was constantly walking around with my head down, like Cousin It from The Addams Family, trying to avoid attention. I was always bumping into things; telegraph poles, railing, even people. My parents were constantly telling me to walk with my head up, but that didn't always work out so well as this next story will explain.

Living in the town of Coleraine we had a large, three story bar called The Plough Inn. One day I was told to wait on my mother. She had to bring me back some new shoes as my old ones had become so scruffy. She didn't understand that's why I liked them; I loved that they were wearing out. When my mother came home with a new pair of very shiny black and white patent leather shoes I thought they were just awful. They glared back at me and made my feet seem huge and prominent, but I had to wear them. Later that day, as I went down the street, I was mindful to walk with my head up for a change. Maybe it helped that I did not want to look at those shoes. I parted my hair a bit, kept my shoulders back and my eyes level. I began to feel a new sense of confidence as I strode through town, but it wasn't until I got home that I noticed that somehow I had walked right through fresh concrete. To this day I really have no idea how I missed it. I only noticed my feet when I was home standing outside the front door. I panicked. The new shoes were ruined and I thought my mother would kill me. I quickly snuck inside and desperately tried to find a place to hide. Suddenly I had what I thought was a great idea. The hot cupboard was where my mother put all the washed and ironed clothes. It contained the hot water tank and would keep all the linens fresh and warm. It was also the perfect place for a seven year old to hide. Climbing up, I wedged myself into the cupboard on the middle shelf and closed the door.

Well there I was, thinking of all the bad things that were going to happen to me when my mother saw what had become of my new shoes. The cupboard got so hot that my hair was plastered to my head. To make matters worse, the concrete hardened and my shoes stuck to the clean sheets. As I sat in my misery, I could hear my parents talking. They had begun to get worried because I wasn't home yet. Still, I stayed put, fearing the repercussions of my shoe escapade. After a while their worry grew more serious and they were going to call the police. I covered my face with my hands, thinking what a disaster it would be. Now the police were going to get involved! I might get arrested, me, a seven year old girl! I was so afraid that I couldn't move. Thank God my father decided that they should search the house first. It wasn't long before the door of the hot cupboard opened and he found me, red cheeked to say the least, with solid blocks of concrete for feet. As my dad lifted me out, the sheets came with me, cemented to my socks and shoes. I was terrified but he just laughed. I tried telling him why I had hid and about putting my head up for a change. This made him laugh even more.

This story is a good illustration of what fear can make us do. It must be the reason we have so many misadventures as children, so we can learn for our future that our fears and worries are all for nothing most of the time. When I look back, this story serves as a lesson to not look too far ahead, be more grounded in the present and watch what pathway we choose.

A Heavenly Gift

While we were living in Coleraine, my father's health began to fail. It was shortly after the cement shoes incident that he took his first heart attack. I remember that he was taken to the hospital and when he came back home he was very tired. He spent a lot of time in bed, which had to be moved into the main sitting room while he recovered. I would hide behind him on the bed while my brothers would watch horror movies in front of the fire. Slowly my father got better, but he knew that he needed a change. Working in the pubs was too much of a strain on him, so my parents decided to move back to Garvaghy, in County Tyrone where my parents had been raised. All of us children were very excited at the news because that's where our granny lived. Over the years, we had many visits to our grandmothers and would often spend whole summers there. When I think of granny I know that she had spiritual gifts of her own. All the children knew that she read tea-leaves for people and the fire for messages, but strangely she would never read for any of us kids.

Granny was a central figure in the community and lived to the age of ninety-eight. I remember people would come over to ask her about local history. She was always willing to share what she knew. Her house was a typical cottage style. The front door opened into the living room while other doors led off to bedrooms and back rooms. It was always cozy and beautiful. Granny and my aunt Mary, the local primary school cook, lived together so there was always fresh baked bread and scones. We loved being sent to do jobs when we where staying like bringing the cows in for milking. Mary and granny would make butter and have fresh buttermilk everyday for baking. There were only two cows but they also had seven or eight hens, two cats, and a fluffy collie dog named Shep. In contrast to town living, Granny's house in the country was total freedom and fun.

One summer, before we moved to live beside granny, we were staying for our holidays. The adults went out leaving Brendan, my oldest brother, to look after us kids for the evening. In his youth Brendan was the practical joker in the family with a mind that must have been filled with mischief. I had gone off to bed after a long day in the fields. Well, this story explains his sense of humour - he knew I was terrified of the cows, especially if they were too close, but he thought it would be hilarious to take a full-grown cow through grannies house and right into my bedroom. That the huge animal didn't break something was a miracle. I'm still not sure how I woke, but when I did I was staring into the face of Granny's big black cow. All I could see was this massive animal's head leaning into me with its big brown eyes and the smell of its grassy, milky breath huffing into my face. And here's me, a small girl, tiny in comparison to a ton of cow! I think I froze, because no words or sound would come out of my mouth. The cow was probably more afraid and confused than me. I backed into the corner and covered my face in shock as it slowly tried to turn, trying to get out of the room. Brendan was doubled over with laughter as I braced for the inevitable crashing and breaking that would come from this massive animal in a tiny room. But astonishingly, the animal calmly turned, walked out and continued on out the front door. I sat there shaking in stunned disbelief, which sent Brendan into further fits of laughter. When I told my parents of the incident, I think they didn't believe me at first, but when Brendan was hauled in and questioned, the truth finally came out. He got a good telling off but I think he found it too hilarious to be bothered. It was such a mad thing to do and could have been much more serious, but as children we never think of the consequences. Clearly my angels were looking out for me that day, but it wasn't the last time Brendan would demonstrate his knack for mad ideas.

As a family of six children, our house was always busy, made even more so by the fact that we lived over bars most of our lives. Still, my parents gave us a great upbringing, doing the normal things families do. We would have treats on Friday nights like fish and chips and walks in the park. Then there was the wonderful two-week holiday we took every year when my parents would take us to Donegal in the summer. I loved being at the beach, the outdoors was where I was happiest.

One of our family trips took us to Bloody Foreland in Donegal. We rented a house on the coast and would go out exploring the area. The scenery in County Donegal is wild and beautiful and we never tired of it. As children living in a town, we loved going out on our explorations of this beautiful place. I was walking at the seashore with my brothers Colin and Brendan. We all started to hear other children laughing. There seemed to be a lot of them. Suddenly we felt showers of what was like small stones being thrown over us from the cliffs above. We looked, but no one was there. We thought we could maybe make some new friends while on holiday, but we could only hear them and no one answered us when we called out. This happened for quite a distance and then it just suddenly stopped. We thought it a little strange and a bit scary. Still, the attention span of children is limited and it wasn't long before we forgot about it and we headed back to the holiday house.

When we got back to the house there was an elderly fisherman chatting to our parents. They had got to know him over the years and he had stopped in for a friendly visit, as people often did in those days. Remarkably, he was telling them about the shoreline at Bloody Foreland being haunted and the strange things people had experienced. As I sat listening I grew more scared by the minute. Being raised not to interrupt adults, we all kept quiet until he had finished his story. He told how spirits haunted the shore. Many ships had sunk off the coast including passenger ships with women and children on board. He said that the spirits of the children could be heard playing on the shore and would sometimes, just for fun, throw pebbles at the living. As he finished his story, we were falling over ourselves to tell our story to them. We had heard and felt exactly what this man described. We stayed away from the beach for the rest of the week, afraid we would encounter the spirit children of the Bloody Foreland coast again. These are two of the earliest experiences of spirit I can remember in my childhood – the sad feeling at the old ruin, and this one in Donegal.

The stories of my brother Brendan in my childhood do stand out because of the fear I felt when they happened. Brendan always seemed to see the fun in scaring me and his creativity knew no bounds. Our Granny loved her clothes and she had a long coat and gloves made from a luxurious, dark, brown fur. She hung a real fox fur over the shoulders; it was the old style fox collar with the tail and face still on it that was the fashion at the time. I was completely afraid of this coat and fox shawl. It was hung behind the door in the bedroom where I slept. I know it sounds ridiculous but it scared me so much I would make sure I passed it quickly and not look at it. One night I had gone to bed and was fast asleep when I woke in the dark to an awful howling and groaning sound from the corner of the room. As my eyes snapped open and adjusted to the dark things became clearer I saw the fur coat, still hanging on the door, flailing and moving wildly. The fur gloves waved and the fox face seemed to glare at me. I screamed so much that by the time my parents ran up, I was hyperventilating. Even when the light went on and Brendan was literally pulled out of the big coat, I keep screaming. It was just too much for child to handle. Brendan, still in the fur gloves and the fox skin dangling from his neck looked ridiculous and was laughing uncontrollably as my father removed him from the room. When I think of it now, it was really funny. We still laugh at the things we did as children. With so many siblings life was never dull. I love them all and we are still very close.

My Aunt and granny were such a vital part of my upbringing. Many years later in my forties I did a reading for a mother and daughter that exemplifies how our grandparents are so connected to us and are such important members of any family. Their wisdom, kindness and love are sometimes not really missed until they have gone from our lives.

When Ann and her daughter Gemma came to me for a reading they really wanted to hear from their family members that had passed on. Ann was much more interested for this to happen than Gemma. The reading for Ann turned out to be very detailed and positive, but for her no one from the spirit realm came through. She was disappointed, but I always let people know before they come along that I do not call or ask spirit to be there. It is up to my angels and guides whether a spirit is permitted to be there for each individual person. Now when Ann's daughter Gemma came in it was entirely different. I could only laugh at what I was being shown. Two elderly ladies were walking towards us in a tunnel of light, but the light that surrounded them was in shades of lilac and purple, it was very beautiful to see. They were linked arm in arm, nattering away like they were out for a dander on a sunny day. They arrived, both with loving smiles in Gemma's direction so I explained to Gemma what I was seeing.

I said, "There are two wonderful ladies here now and they are both your grannies."

Gemma said, " Oh my God, yes both my grannies died within a short time of each other and they had been really great friends as well."

I was then guided to mention the colours of their clothes because it was important to the family. I carried on telling Gemma, "The two ladies are wearing suits; one lilac and one purple and they are both called Margaret."

Gemma gasped and then laughed. I was feeling a little doubtful of the correct names because the chances of both of them being called Margaret was rare in my experience. But Gemma explained to me that each granny was indeed called Margaret and that they had requested before they died that one wanted to be buried in her favourite lilac suit, and the other in her favourite purple suit. The family had thought this an unusual request from each of them when they where alive, but they insisted that it be that way. It was a detail that was very specific and gave total validation on this occasion. So here they were, standing in front of us and letting Gemma know that it was indeed her two grannies. She got the message of validation so many want to hear; that they are so happy and thrilled to be allowed to come through and see their family again, they have no illness or pain, it simply does not exist anymore for them. They made it clear that they were bringing messages of love to everyone and that when anyone in the family needed help, just ask them through prayers or a heartfelt plea and they would answer in some way.

Every time we talk to our deceased family members or pray for help they pray with you in spirit form with your guardian angel to God. It is so powerful that people need to realise they should be doing it more often. The details of colours and names were so much of a testimony for Gemma. She was a little shocked to say the least. I felt it was a wonderful gift for the family and gave them a great feeling of happiness to know they were together and so present and joyful.

Gemma had no expectations about her reading, which was helpful. It's easier to connect to the spirit world if the person getting the reading is in a very relaxed state. Ann, her mother, had been emotional and had really wanted to connect and had not been able to. I feel that perhaps her need for that to happen had closed that door to her. I always realise what a special gift it is to have a loved one be brought through to say hello. It is an amazing energy when it happens and it always leaves a feeling of calmness hope and peace.

Pauline Johnson

CHAPTER 2
Life & Loss

I went to my first school in Stewartstown. I never particularly liked school. I always wanted to be free and hated being put into the school knowing I was stuck there until three o'clock. We moved quite a lot so we changed schools quite a bit. It was difficult to form friendships and feel grounded in one place with us moving all the time. We would make friends and then have to move again so, without many friends I turned to books. I loved to read and it really helped to ground me. I would devour books, particularly ghost stories, to my mother's amusement. I would get engrossed in a book for days. It was the part of school that I liked, all the endless new books to read.

We moved from Stewartstown to the town of Coleraine. We then developed some great friendships and the school was suddenly much more tolerable, but after five years, once again, we had to face another move. Leaving Coleraine was not easy and though the difficulty was offset by the fact that we were going to live in the countryside, we were not looking forward to the new school. But it was wonderful when we knew we would finally be moving to live next to granny. This was the time we started to live in County Tyrone. Dad started a business raising poultry on a large scale. The main poultry building was over a hundred feet long and sixty feet wide. It was built next to our house along with several other sheds, but it meant that dad didn't have to leave home to go to work, so we always had more time with him. Though it was easier than working in the pubs, the work was still hard. We all had little jobs to do though Brendan did a lot of the work as he was the oldest. Nigel and Garry were only toddlers, Colin and I would get wee jobs to do and Carmel my sister was in school as well. During this time, my father was struck with another heart attack. He was told he had been clinically dead for over five minutes this time around. I was only about nine years old. I remember it was just after he got out of the hospital and we were all out for dinner. Right in the middle of dinner conversation I asked him if he had seen a light or anything when he died. I really don't know where the question came from at the time.

My mother gave me a disapproving look but my father just laughed and said, "I didn't see anything Pauline."

When I think back now it was a strange question for me to ask then as it was not something I knew anything about. I believe that I was being told, even at nine years old, that spirituality would be something that I would have more than just a passing interest in.

Our new school in County Tyrone was so much smaller than our old school in Coleraine. The old school in Coleraine had over six hundred kids, the new school had only sixty. They were a tight-knit group and I think they found it hard to welcome outsiders. Starting my third primary school was not easy. There was a boy in my new class who bullied me nearly every day. He would write the most awful pornographic notes that no child should have knowledge of at nine or ten years old. I certainly didn't understand the notes at the time but I eventually took some of the note's home and showed them to my father. He started to read them and I watched as his face went from concern to anger.

I thought I had done something awful, but he said, "This is not anything to do with you Pauline. We will be going over to the school to sort this out."

I was in a state of terror, as any child would be that doesn't feel accepted at a new school, but the thought of my parents having to go to the school because of me was awful. I hated the thought of having attention focused on me as it was bad enough already. I'm sure my father had some sharp words with the teachers at the school because immediately after the visit the notes ended to my great relief. However, my challenges at the new school were far from over.

A Heavenly Gift

A lot of schools in Northern Ireland require the students to wear uniforms. Fashion has a way of identifying social class and when the kids are all wearing the same thing it eliminates that kind of discrimination. Unfortunately, the new school didn't have that policy and, being from a different area, my clothes were different than the other kids. There were more than a few occasions that the teacher I had at that time would bring me up in front of the class and ask the other pupils what they thought of what I was wearing that day. This would happen often to my dismay. This teacher was not happy that I had come from a school in Coleraine and that what I had been taught was a bit ahead of my class. She would hit me on the knuckles with the wooden part of the blackboard duster if I wrote in 'joined' or 'cursive' writing. The other pupils there had only been taught to write in a print form. I found this totally confusing and despite the punishment, I helped some of the other students learn to write in cursive on my breaks. Still, every day I could not wait to just get home though I had to take measures to hide my red knuckles from my parents. This continued for a while, but eventually the day came when my dad discovered the truth and my parents had to go back to the school to get things sorted out all over again.

My primary school teacher was mean and nasty at times and as a child I couldn't figure out why. A child should never have to worry or deal with this type of situation from a teacher. It was completely overwhelming and added to my growing disdain for school. In contrast, life at our new home was wonderful. We loved the countryside with the beautiful fields and streams. It gave us a feeling of being unlimited and free to explore. On Sundays, our cousins would come over and there would be a great crowd of us kids playing football in one of the fields to the front of Grannies house. One Sunday we were all out as usual and I ran to get the ball. The ball just seemed to roll and roll away from me. By the time I reached it, I was close to the old well. The well had always been there, it was down a steep bank at the far end of the field. A small path lead down to it, it was really just a hole in the ground, surrounded by bricks with the water lapping up over the sides. Reaching down to pick up the ball, I looked down to the well just in time to see two small children hands slipping off the edge.

It was my youngest brother Nigel, he was just starting to float face down in the well. He was only about three years old and had somehow managed to wander off on his own. The water in the well was about four feet deep and Nigel's head was going under. He had hit his face when he fell and his wee hands just couldn't hold on any longer. The ball was forgotten and I jumped down the six feet slope to the well. I still don't know how I lifted Nigel out by myself. He had a duffle coat on, and it was logged with water at this stage. Somehow I managed to gather him up and carry him all the way back to the house, half running and half walking.

After that the evening was a blur. Nigel was rushed to the hospital and checked out and to our astonishment he was fine. If that ball had not have rolled in the direction of the well, my wonderful brother Nigel would not be here today. It's a story of how heaven works. We are nudged in the right direction and given help everyday to guide, help and protect ourselves and others. I am so glad I was put in that place just at the most needed moment. If not, it would have been such a tragic and terrible loss.

Primary school at this time was still an issue. The visits from my dad had stopped the boy from writing me those awful letters, but it took intervention from my brother Colin, standing up to the bullying antics that finally put an end to it all. I have amazing brothers, and a sister that I am so blessed to have. Shortly after that I was off to Secondary school, what they call High School now in some places. At the time it seemed that Primary school would never end for me, but everything changes eventually though some changes seem to turn the world upside down. I was thirteen years old and settling into my new school when dad had another heart attack. This one was different, much stronger and the ambulance had to come and take him to the hospital. We all thought he would be home again soon as usual. I still remember the ambulance door being closed as he weakly lifted his hand to wave goodbye to us.

The phone call came to our house and he died on the Sunday morning. It was devastating. I loved my father so much. He was such a loving, kind, wonderful man. I thought, *He can't, leave! What about us, what do we do without him?* I went completely numb. I didn't even cry. I would do that much later on though, and when I did, it would hit like waves, on and off. The days ahead were a blur. We have wakes in Ireland. Now that I am older, I believe wakes are a healthy tradition and a great comfort to the ones left behind, but when it was my own father, it seemed surreal. To look at him in the coffin and know that he wasn't ever going to wake up, or ever feel warm to me again, or have him smile or hug me was such a deep sadness and I knew we all felt the same. My younger brothers came in on the day of the funeral. They were so small then, I could hardly watch them looking at my father lying in the coffin. They kept asking, "Why isn't daddy waking up?" Looking to each of us for an answer. I had no words that would take away the bewildered look on their wee faces. I had to walk away.

The crowds of people that came to my father's wake were wonderful. It was such a hard time for all of us. My mother was only thirty-nine years old at the time, with my three brothers still under ten years old; my youngest brother Nigel was so tiny. My mother is a very strong person and had to look after all of us. Life at this point changed quite a bit. It was very bleak at times. The absence of my father's huge loving presence left us feeling hollow and empty, but it was shortly after this time that I started to sense he was still there with us.

Sometimes strong emotions can overwhelm our ability to sense the subtle connection with our deceased loved ones and our angels and guides. It is something I had to learn to control to do my work. Years later I had a client named Gwen who experienced this first hand.

Gwen is a beautiful girl in her twenties, good at her job with lots of friends. Her cousin Victoria was like a little sister that Gwen never had. These two were practically joined at the hip and they did everything together. Shortly before Gwen had come to me I read in the local paper of a terrible car accident in which two young people had lost their lives. When Gwen booked to come and see me a week after I read this sad news, the article came into my mind. I thought this girl is somehow related to this newspaper story. Gwen arrived and within a few minutes the angels and guides let me know that Gwen had suffered a terrible loss the week before and that her cousin Victoria was one of the young people that had died in the car accident I had read about. I could see the anguish that Gwen was going through. I knew she could find no comfort or release from the hurt she was going through at this time. Gwen told me how she believed in God and the angels and that she had her own collection of angel figurines at home, but she could find no peace. She told me about Victoria and how close they had been and she was finding it hard to deal with the constant battle inside her mind of why Victoria was taken from her and her family. Victoria and her boyfriend had both been killed in the accident. Poor Gwen had lost two of the people closest to her.

While Gwen was telling me about how much she was dealing with, my guides brought a beautiful young woman from spirit into the room. This girl radiated dazzling light and was wearing a long white flowing dress. I told Gwen that a girl about her age was with us and that she was pointing to her neck area. I suddenly got this sharp pain across my own neck and she continued to show me her head falling to the side. It fell to a disturbing, unnatural angle and her face had a blank expression. It took me a short time to relay this to Gwen as gently as I could. I told her that this girl had broken her neck and that her head had fallen to the right where I was shown her injuries had been. It had been an instant death. I did not know the details of how Victoria had died, but when I explained to Gwen what I was being shown she just knew it was Victoria that was with us.

Gwen sat quietly crying for a time while I tried to comfort her. Gwen told me how they had been told the details of Victoria's death and that she had indeed broken her neck and her injuries were mostly on the right side. At this point I was knew that this was indeed the girl I had read about in the paper the previous week, as her facial features were not made clear to me. This beautiful girl in spirit now changed and was smiling at me. She looked incredibly alive, happy and strong. I was guided to tell Gwen that Victoria was not in any pain whatsoever and was in the loving light of Heaven where she will be a light to help and guide Gwen on earth when she needed her. Gwen knew that her frustration, pain and sadness were because she was still in the early stages of grieving, but it can still be very difficult to deal with such loss even when you are reassured that your loved ones are safe and happy in Heaven. Victoria coming through to Gwen had released some of the feeling of loss but healing takes time and it can be very different for each person. For Gwen it was all so sudden and devastating, but she did say it made her happy to know Victoria was in a beautiful place. Still, she wanted her to be on earth with her. Gwen is still dealing with the the difficulty of it all. Life is beautiful but it can be rough, especially when young people pass. It leaves us with many unanswered questions. The angels want us to know that they are always here to help and for us to anchor ourselves to that light and hope no matter how shattering the circumstances can be.

Rebecca was in her sixties and was an American living in Ireland, and had lost her husband a year before she came to me. Rebecca is a very creative person and would make pottery with her husband while he had been alive. They had been together for forty years and she was so lost after he passed. She tried to have some sort of routine to fill her days but was still having such a hard time losing the man she had shared her life with. She loved her dogs and would go for long walks on the beach near her home. Rebecca explained to me that she had met her husband in America in the sixties while she was there on holiday and had very quickly fallen in love. They decided to make it permanent and she moved all the way from New York to Ireland where they had such a happy life together for all the years that were to come. But when her husband had died quite suddenly it was an enormous shock for her.

When the angels and guides arrived to help Rebecca they came with a beautiful soft warm energy as they always do. They also brought her deceased husband with them. Rebecca looked at me with a look of total wonder on her face as she said how she felt like she was being hugged. To her it was like a hug she would have had from her husband. It was a lot for her to take in as she had been carrying the sadness of the reality that he was now gone from her. I was guided to let her know that she is never alone and that she has only to ask for help and that she would indeed receive what she needed. I also explained to her that I was being shown a room with cream-painted shelves and beautiful pale-blue pottery displayed on each shelf. I was told to let her know that her husband does still visit their home and to have the belief and trust that he does. She was to talk to him because he was never far away and to start to realise that she would know when he was there for a quick visit. Rebecca was so surprised that I could tell her about the shelves and the pottery because that was indeed the truth. Her husband had painted the shelves in a cream colour before he had died and the pottery they made together was all displayed on them. She was guided to not forget her gifts for making pottery and to fill her days with beauty and happiness. Her deceased husband did not want her to drag herself through each day but to embrace life as they had always done together. She was also told that her sadness would soon lift for the first time in nearly a year and that her health would improve with that. Rebecca was more than a little energised when her visit to me had ended. She explained that she felt giddy and light and that it was hard for her to put into words how she felt. She had gone through an array of emotions while she was with me. She said she had felt sad, shocked, happy and exhilarated all within an hour, she could only laugh when she was telling me all this. I could see the bright light return to her face and eyes, it was that wonderful light of hope returning. Rebecca left that day with a need to start living life again and seeing it not as something she had to endure but something she was blessed to be doing. Our loved ones may be gone from us in an earthly sense, but they continue on in spirit. The love we share with them never dies, never stops, and is never wasted.

A Heavenly Gift

Pauline Johnson

CHAPTER 3
Senses & Sight

After the death of my father, things at home were very hard. We all struggled in our own way and I couldn't wait to leave school and start work just to be doing something to move forward. It was at this time I could sense a presence in the house, especially at night. At first I thought I was imagining it, but shortly after going to sleep I would wake to a feeling of weight on the bed. After this had happened several times I deliberately stayed awake, to make sure I wasn't dreaming it. Sure enough, as I lay in bed, I actually watched as the blankets were tucked in around me. I was paralysed with fear. When it stopped, I literally ran out of the bedroom. My mother had not gone to bed yet so I told her about what had happened. She looked at me like I was mad, but nothing would get me to sleep in the room for a week. When I finally went back, the same thing happened again.

This time I woke from a deep sleep, and being fuzzy headed thought it was just my dad tucking me in like he used to do. As my head began to clear, this knowledge stayed with me and the sense of fear was replaced by a wonderful calm feeling. The feeling of dread was totally gone, only a feeling of being looked after and loved remained with me. When I told my mother it had happened again, to my surprise she said it had started to happen to her. She too knew it was my father. It still happens at different times to this day. This was my first experience of spirit activity manifesting in physical form and it was comforting as it was my own dad. But I still wanted him to be here with us. As a child I missed him more than I could stand. Losing a parent is a devastating torment for children. It takes years to heal and years to move forward from such a loss. It is an early realisation in a child's life that nothing is permanent and that even the most needed and strongest person that makes you feel secure can be taken away in a blink. It leaves a sense of fear that can be crippling and terrifying at such an early age, and can manifest as destructive behaviour later in life. At least that was how it was for me; looking for security and strength from others and carrying the dread of losing them. The experience and the feeling of him still being with me after he died was incredible and so comforting. It helped me, but it was not easy to live every day without seeing him and having his presence in our lives.

Six months after the death of my father I started dating. It felt better at times to be away from home than to be there. Being home reminded me that my father was gone. I think all of us felt the same, but my family has great faith. As Catholics, we went to mass every Sunday. It anchored us together, reassured us that dad was in a wonderful place and gave us a sense of peace and the strength to carry on.

Everything seemed to be progressing so quickly after the death of my dad. I had gone from being thirteen years old when he died and was now sixteen years old. I just wanted to be working, earning some money to be able to help at home. My three younger brothers were still at school, and my older brother Brendan was trying his best to keep the poultry farm going with my mum. My older sister, Carmel had started her nursing career and had to be away a lot working long hours.

I got my first job in a clothes store in Omagh where I was paid fifteen pounds a week. It was so great to be bringing home some money of my own, but the job didn't last very long. Soon I picked up a new job working in a grocery store. I really enjoyed it, but it was hard work. My shift was from eight thirty in the morning till nine in the evening, four days a week, and on a Saturday, from nine till five thirty. For this I got paid thirty pounds a week, not a lot but it was something. I would hitchhike to work and get a lift home in the evenings. I was usually totally exhausted by Sunday and I began to battle with illness. I would get bad chest infections, earaches, and a terrible pain at the back of my neck that would put me in tears from the pain. Finally I couldn't take the sleepless nights any more and went to the doctor where I was diagnosed with glandular fever. One of the symptoms was that I was totally exhausted and needed a lot of sleep. I didn't get over this for three years. In the end, I had a terrible flu and lost a serious amount of weight. Even drinking water made me sick. I prayed a lot to get better and my health slowly returned. We would pray the rosary as a family and I prayed the rosary to get healthy every day at this time, I also pray this prayer for everyone I do readings for now and their families it is a very powerful beautiful prayer to do.

My boyfriend and I got engaged when I was 17 years old and he was 24. It wasn't a fancy, romantic engagement. There was no proposal, there wasn't even an engagement party or celebration of any kind. It happened while we were going to Dublin on a work trip. We stopped in Dundalk, and we called into Penny's shopping centre and he called me into a jewellery shop. I went in and he said, "Pick one". I looked at the girl in the shop and then at the selection of rings. I didn't realise in that moment that they were engagement rings. I didn't feel ready or dressed for the occasion, I had on jeans and a jumper. I picked a ring that looked like a flower and that was that. I was engaged. This was a time in my life where spiritual things were not on my mind at all. It was more about travel, going out and having fun, my boyfriend and working.

We traveled a lot together before we got married and afterwards as well. We visited, Cyprus, Greece, Italy, Austria, Germany, France, Dubai, Maldives, and many more wonderful places. The first time I drank alcohol I was in Greece in Corfu and I remember it as clear as day; it was a tequila sunrise. It looked exotic and unusual, red and orange with a little umbrella and tasted great. I had three of them and it was three too many. I remember I was sitting on a wall one minute and the next, I had fallen backwards and was looking up at my feet. I must have looked hilarious. There was a thunderstorm going on and in the middle of all that I had to be carried home. How embarrassing! I have never been much of a drinker and only have an odd drink now. I didn't know at the time that I have a terrible allergy to anything orange so that didn't help either but it's always good to be able to laugh at our own silliness. There's an old saying I like: 'Angels can fly because they take themselves lightly'. This saying teaches so much about our thoughts of self-importance and worry. Laughter is the best medicine to lighten our bodies and minds and we do all need to play and have fun in our lives no matter what our age.

I worked in the grocery shop job for two years and then got a new job working in a chemist shop in Omagh. I also joined a pop-rock band and would be out playing in different venues at the weekends because I have always loved to sing. It was hectic doing the two jobs but I didn't mind. I made new friends and really enjoyed the work, but because I was still hitchhiking to work I did meet some unsavoury characters.

One day in particular I had taken a lift from a man and while he was driving he turned and said, "I want you to spare me fifteen or twenty minutes of your time."

I thought, *Did I just hear that*? Then he said it again. I sat very quiet, I knew I desperately needed to get out of that car. The thought of being raped or attacked had never entered my head ever until this moment. The thought made me feel physically sick but also incredibly angry. I tried to appear unfazed as I searched for a way out of my predicament. It was then I noticed a handgun under the driver seat. My heart sank and the feeling of fear formed a fist in the pit of my stomach. It was in the days of the troubles in Northern Ireland so I knew that guns where in existence, but to actually see a gun this close was terrifying. I reached for the door handle, I didn't care if the car was moving at speed, I was getting out. Just then he slammed on the brakes and I was flung forward. I barely managed to get my hands on the dash to catch myself. Thankfully, when he did this the car stalled giving me an opportunity to go for the door handle. He lunged across the seat to grab me, but I put my knee up, pushed his arm away and managed to get out of the car. I don't know where I got the strength. It was like a sense of calm determination came over me. I think because I was more angry than afraid, I just started walking on the road.

He drove along side me in the car at a crawling speed as I walked away. I thought he was going to shoot me, but then it occurred to me that if he was going to do that, he would probably have at least threatened me with that by now. Just then another car came along the road and I waved them down. I didn't care who it was, I just wanted away from there. Thankfully, they stopped and I escaped with my life. I was so afraid that I did not think of mentioning this incident to anyone. A few months later, a man was arrested for trying the same thing with a girl hitchhiking in the same area. I don't know for sure if it was the same guy, but I know that I was blessed to have gotten away.

I learned an important lesson that day; be strong in fearful situations and try to stay calm. Our fears can manifest right in front of us. The energy we put with our thoughts and words are much more powerful than we realise. If I had not taken the angry approach this outcome would have been completely different. I had been worried about taking lifts with strangers from work and had been dwelling on it far too much at that particular time. We all have the power to manifest things. I chose after this to become much stronger and less fearful. It is something that

I have to work on to this day to keep moving forward.

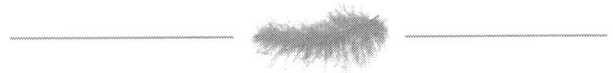

It reminds me of a woman named Maureen who came to me for answers. When Maureen arrived her worries were focused on her daughter. Like a lot of mothers, when your children have problems you want to take them on or try to take them away. In this case, what the daughter was going through had much more to do with how and what her mother was doing in her life. Maureen was very interested in spiritual work and she really enjoyed going to psychic fairs and mediums. To her it was extremely entertaining and she was learning more about spiritual issues. Her daughter Samantha was intelligent and excelled in English and chemistry and had a string of passes in exams to prove it. But Sam's winning ways began to change suddenly when she started to hang out with the wrong groups of friends. She dyed her hair jet black, refused to get out of bed most days and fought with her mother over seemingly trivial things. When Maureen came to me, she was at her wits end to say the least. Maureen had other things happening in her life but her main concern was for Sam.

When she arrived, I began to get the familiar tingling sensation as Serena, my guardian angel brought Maureen's grandmother through. The message from her granny was beautiful and for her to be strong and loving towards her daughter. Maureen is a beautiful, strong person anyway and it was just a little bit of advice to help her realise how much her powerful loving energy would have on the situation. The angels and guides also pointed out to Maureen that she had gone to so many spiritual places to look for answers that she had taken on some negative energy from doing that. Maureen was made aware that her daughter was very sensitive to these energies and that they affected Sam's emotional state in a strong way. Maureen was shocked. She hadn't realised how psychically attuned her daughter was. In addition to the negative energies, Sam was empathising with her mother's emotional state as well. I felt the gentle nudge of Serena as I was guided to ask what Maureen had taken back to her house in the form of spiritual items. Maureen was a little shaken when I asked her this question and as she explained to me what she had done only a few weeks earlier.

Maureen had received an item, I won't go into the details of it here, but she was told to put this item near her daughter in her room and that it was supposed to heal her. She had also purchased other supposed 'healing items' and put these into her daughter's room as well. I was instructed to tell Maureen that, in order to help Sam, she had to remove the item and any other objects, such as crystals and the like, in Sam's room and wash them in salt water to purify them. My guardian angel, Serena also pointed out to Maureen to clear and air out Sam's bedroom. It would get rid of the negative build up of energy that had caused Sam so much turmoil. The angels also asked Maureen to pray for healing for her and her daughter in a way only a mother can do, and that it was ok to return the items to her daughter's new cleared and cleansed room.

As I am writing this story, I am being told that the angels and guides want mothers to realise the incredible powerful and beautiful energy they have in the family unit, and to use it in a warm loving gentle way as Maureen was doing. Maureen asked me at the end of the visit if her daughter could come to see me. I told her that I only do readings for people over eighteen, so she would have to wait for another six months. Maureen felt bad thinking that it was her actions that had brought discord into the family because of places, people and things she had been in contact with, but it was not Maureen's fault.

    I was so pleased to hear from Maureen three months later. She was excited and explained that she had done all the things that had been asked of her. The change in her daughter was so wonderful that Maureen said she was like a totally different girl. Within the first month after Maureen' visit Sam was back to her old self. She was doing really well at school the dyed hair had gone and was back to her natural beautiful auburn colour. She had become involved with a school group to help children in need and was hoping to spend her summer holidays working and being involved with helping kids. Maureen said she was so delighted with the change and just had to let me know that they had gone back to having a close mother-daughter relationship again.

Three months later I got to meet Sam in person. Her mother had given her a voucher from me for her birthday and on the day she turned eighteen, she walked into my reading room. Sam is a sensitive, warm, beautiful girl and shone with the most amazing energy that day. She explained to me that she had felt like she had a dark veil hanging over her, but it was now all gone. She also mentioned how she had received such a new zest for life and no longer felt so tired. All the negativity had left her. I told her to always call on her guardian angel and guides to help her with everything. She is doing really well since and I know she has a lot of amazing adventures ahead of her as she lives her life in service to others. Maureen is a beautiful person inside and out and has also moved on in a wonderful way. Her personal life and family relationships have improved and show no sign of stopping.

It is important to know that it is possible to unintentionally pick up, carry and transmit dark energies. Many people who have energetic sensitivities or psychic gifts aren't even aware of it. But prayer to God and help from the angels of his love and light are the only perfect protection. If you have an interest in doing spiritual work to help others this is the most important thing for you to know. Even if you have nothing to do with spiritual work it is important to protect yourself at times from what other people are involved in. Being made aware and living in a good way is protective in itself. Knowing you walk with such beauty and love from your guardian angel every day is incredible. Of course your prayers don't have to be perfect. Prayers differ from person to person, sometimes the simpler it is, the better.

It was 1985 and my job as lead singer in the band was great fun. I sang in the local choir as well and loved that too. It was an exciting time for music and the band was doing well. We played all around Ireland which kept it interesting and busy. I was twenty-one at the time and driving home from a gig one night when I had an encounter with a spirit around the old house where I had sensed things before when I was seven years old. My brother Brendan had a job with the band as a roadie. He was at the wheel that night, driving on the A5 from Omagh, it was about four o'clock in the morning. We were just coming to where the old ruin of the house was. On the left I noticed what I thought was a person walking towards the road. Just as I was about to tell my brother about what I was seeing the guy appeared right in front of the car, the car lights fully on him. In that flash of an instant he looked straight at me. He was so clear, tall but hunched, his clothes looked like they were animal skins, a prehistoric man but his face was deformed. We drove straight through him like he was mist.

Brendan slammed on the brakes and the car slid to a stop.

"Did you see that?" He stammered. "I just drove straight through someone or…something!"

Brendan's face looked so shocked and he was shaking. He jumped out of the car and ran back to the scene. I was sitting in the car, completely terrified. Brendan came back totally bewildered.

"There's nobody there."

We were both shocked to say the least. He was the first deceased person I had ever seen in front of me. It was a sign of things to come. The next day we went back to the scene, but all we found was our tyre marks. This was the first time that someone I was with had also seen the spirit of the deceased it was not to be the last. Years later I asked the Angels about how we both saw the spirit and I was told that the other person sees the same as I do because I feel afraid. The fear acts as a strong emotional conduit and enables the person I'm with to see what I am seeing. This would happen again with others.

I was still working in the chemist during the day, and performing with the band at night. We ended up in RTE studios in Dublin, on the talent show called Screen Test it was a bit like the X-Factor talent show of today. It was so funny to me to be standing in front of cameras singing, but it was a great experience. We came second in the show, which was quite good at the time. Shortly after this, the band was heading home after another gig. We were all piled into a van with the equipment and most of us were sleeping. For some reason I woke from my sleep and got up. I could see we were driving in dense fog and I put my hand on Charlie's the drivers shoulder. Somehow I just knew to say, "Charlie watch out." Suddenly, a car appeared out of the fog from a side road. Charlie barely had time to swerve a little, but the weight of the van with all the music gear connected with the car. Many people are familiar with the bone-shaking crunch of a car accident and the way that time slows down. I was positioned in the back between the front seats, but was flying forward and just knew I was going through the windscreen. Just as I had that thought, the van rolled and I was twisted in a different direction. Broken glass flew across my face, but when all the awful noise and confusion stopped I lay in the corner of the windscreen, sitting on the dashboard, looking up at Alan and Charlie above me still buckled into their seats. I looked to my left and I was nearly eye level with the road. Shaking the glass from my hair and ears, I stepped out on to the road and stood up. I was okay. I had a stress injury to my back, but other than that, I was fine. I just know that at this time, the angels had woken me and made me warn Charlie. I was protected and looked after through the whole event. No one in the band suffered any injuries. We were badly shaken to say the least but that was all, which was incredible considering all of the heavy equipment that had been thrown around in the back. The roof had nearly been torn off the car that had pulled out in front of us, but the girl in the car had been very lucky to survive. She had been drinking alcohol and driving. The ambulance came and she was treated at the hospital for a cut on her head.

    Our angels often take measures to protect and warn us of impending danger and lessen the severity of accidents when they happen. This was a prime example of them doing just that.

Pauline Johnson

CHAPTER 4

Paradox of Perfection

My fiancé did not want me to be in the band when we were married so I had to leave that behind. I wanted to get married on August 20th the following year, but it did not work out for that date. Twenty years later in my life though I would meet a very special person on that exact date the 20th of August, only it would be six thousand miles away from Ireland. But for now I had my wedding on the seventh August 1986 instead.

After a lot of the normal fuss and bother the wedding day finally arrived. I am not particularly fond of weddings and my own wedding brought no change to that feeling. Even though I was the one getting married, I was pensive. I would have liked a quiet wedding and an intimate gathering, but it turned out to be quite a big wedding. I put thought into my wedding dress, it is a custom that the style of the wedding dress is a bit of a secret. There was enough stress about the day without drama two weeks before the wedding. A female relative of my fiancé went and viewed my dress without telling me, and then telephoned me to say that the priest had not married a couple because her dress was similar to mine. I was so shocked that someone would think this way, but the more I thought about it, the more I decided not to change the dress because of another person's opinion. It was a hard lesson for me, being young and of low self-esteem I didn't think I could say anything or confront this person because of a family connection. I saw others as being more intelligent, more important, and more knowing in general. I was not very aware at this time of how the dark and negative energies work through people that were close to me. I worried so much about this dress and what might be said to me that it took some of the enjoyment away when I put it on the morning of the wedding. This lesson was to be repeated, again and again in my life until I started to trust myself, and not worry of what others thought or said in a negative way at important times in my life.

I think people get lost in silly details of weddings instead of what it's really about; two people making a blessed contract on earth because of their love for each other and celebrating that. As the bible quote goes:

[Matthew 16:19]
"I tell you the truth, whatever you bind on earth will be bound in heaven, and whatever you loose on earth will be loosed in heaven."

This quote came to mind many years later as events unfolded in my life. The day of the wedding, I had such a feeling of thoughtfulness, and it would not go away. There were certain things that I had my doubts about, but what I felt for my fiancé was real and true. I was totally in love with him. Still, things niggled at me all that morning while

I was getting ready. I got into the car to go to the chapel and we were off.

I was so nervous standing outside the door of the chapel, and then we stepped inside. All I could see were faces turned my way and suddenly my brother said, "Put your foot forward." I didn't realise I had frozen to the spot. I was in a bit of a daze to say the least. The chapel was beautiful, all lit up and done with white ribbons and flowers the day before. I could feel tears running down my face, but did not really know why I was crying. I had just put my foot forward and had started to walk up the aisle when all the lights went out and the music stopped. It was totally dark apart from the altar candles. The electricity had gone off in the chapel. The silence was deafening and I could hear my own heartbeat and my footsteps echo off the walls. Eventually someone got a generator running outside at the back of the chapel. The noise was so loud it was comical. What a start to a wedding! Later in my life I would experience the effects that my strong emotions would have on electrical appliances and lights. The rest of the day went off quite well, it was like a blur. I was glad when the day came to an end as I was exhausted.

So my married life began. We moved into the beautiful new house we had built, address number nine. I had just left my mother's and her address was one nine seven. These numbers have constantly reoccurred in my life and are quite important as you will read more about a little later. I started working with my husband in the office. I was always conscientious about my work and would try to do it well. There was always plenty to do both in the office and at home, but I loved our home and loved working so close by.

At the start of my marriage, I would very much go with the flow of things. We took a holiday each year for two weeks, and it was wonderful. I immersed myself in his life. We worked together, lived together and spent most of our leisure time with his family members but I enjoyed all of it. I was always aware of how I looked, and how I thought I should look, and would worry about my weight quite a bit. I thought I had to try hard to fit in and to be accepted, it was all very draining. It took way more energy to be in a negative state of mind about myself than a positive one, but I didn't see at this time how hard I was being on myself.

I enjoy cooking as well and would spend quite a bit of time preparing an evening dinner for any friends we would invite over. I loved taking time to make things look beautiful should it be food or our home it was a creative outlet for me. We would visit other people's homes and have people over on most weekends, but it only takes a few words to change things. Like I mentioned earlier about the effect of other's opinions.

"You would be perfect if you lost that bit of weight." He would say to me.

These particular words just sat in my mind like they were stuck, and then they started to grow. That's when I began having problems with eating. I thought I need to be thinner. If I could lose weight I would be more loved and I would be a better person. This was the start of lots of changes to come. I think I was around 26 years old and I started to eat less and less. Eventually I was just having a bowl of porridge a day with some tea and water. It's strange how an eating disorder creeps in and slowly gets worse. It became so bad that when food was put in front of me, the look of it would make me feel sick. To eat it felt like I was swallowing stones. I was also doing vigorous exercise at least three or four times a week. Swimming, walking, lifting weights, doing anything to work off the tiny bit of food I had eaten. I had been easy going, relaxed and loved a good laugh. Now I wanted to withdraw, to be alone and not let anyone see that I was not eating, or that if I did eat, I had to throw it up. I became isolated from family and friends. I started to feel so unwell and was always totally exhausted. I was completely focused on my weight and how I looked while any confidence I had completely disappeared. My moods were all over the place. I didn't want to go out or be seen. I could not speak to anyone about this as I was feeling so low, miserable, secretive, weak and alone in this self conscious paranoid state. My hair started to fall out in handfuls every time I combed it. My nails where cracking and the cramping pain throughout my body at times was unbearable, it felt like knives stabbing my body from every angle. Still I carried on, and ended up sleeping more and more in the day. I had no energy whatsoever and was not interested in being social or mixing with people because I felt so listless, and I certainly did not want people to notice me or mention my weight.

It didn't help at this time that three of my brothers had been working in England and I had not seen them for a few years. They all came home for Christmas and I answered the door when they arrived. I'll never forget the look on my brother Colin's face. Colin is a person that always says what he thinks and the first thing he said was, "What's wrong with you, are you sick?" Then Garry and Brendan arrived and I got looks from both of them, but nothing was said. To me, I didn't think I looked that different.

I was also starting to have vivid dreams, and a few days later these things would actually happen. In the first dream I was in a car and it was following another car at a very fast speed on a dark, foggy night. I followed the car around a bad bend in the road, suddenly we were flying over a hedge and falling after the first car. I jumped in my bed, drenched in sweat. I woke my husband and said, "There's been an accident." He dismissed it as a bad dream, but the next day all the details of the dream were still vivid. It was four days later that the accident actually happened.

My husband's brother was driving in the fog, following his friend's car and both cars went off the road on a bad corner. We got the phone call to go and help. When I got to the scene it was just like I had dreamt; the fog, the road, and the bend. Luckily everyone was okay, but my husband was looking at me like I was a bit strange because of the detail I had told him of in the dream four days earlier.

The second dream was not long after this. Again I woke out of a nightmare, panicking. I was watching a person's hand using an ATM machine with a card that I knew had been stolen. It was a male hand and he counted out five hundred pounds. When I told my husband about the dream, again he thought I was going mad but I had to check my bank cards, even though it was three o'clock in the morning I knew it was important. My cards were fine, but a few days later my husband's sister had her card stolen and five hundred pounds was taken from her account.

I had no idea why I was getting these dreams about other people. It didn't make sense to me at all, but I began to pay more attention to my dreams, which have now become an important way for me to receive messages from my angels and guides. At the same time of these dreams I also heard an incredible high-pitched sound. This happened while I was sleeping but it was so intense that I woke and was even a little deaf for a short time afterwards. I have heard this sound only twice in my life. Later I found out what it was and what it meant. Up until this time I hadn't become fully aware of my gifts. My mind was too busy with daft things like my appearance or how the house looked. To me everything needing to be perfect all the time was the most important thing. To me, not eating was a way of making things better and it was something I could control, but the truth was, not eating was making me wired. It was like my mind was going at warp speed and my body was getting weaker just trying to keep up.

A Heavenly Gift

It was around this time we decided we would go to Austria on holiday to the beautiful village of Saalbach. As we had never driven in Europe we opted to drive instead of fly just for a bit of an adventure. The drive was spectacular and we arrived on a Saturday to Saalbach and got settled into our hotel. It was the Salzeburgerhof hotel right in the middle of the village. The village dates back to 1222 and is very quaint and beautiful with a charming old church in the square and Edelweiss flowers everywhere. Just two days into the trip we both decided we would do one of the many walks they had marked out for us.

We got everything sorted out including a packed lunch and started to walk from the hotel. It was a beautiful day and we had headed out in the morning about ten o'clock. Suddenly, to my right as I walked, there was a man walking in step with me so close I should have felt him brush my arm. As I turned to look at him, he abruptly stopped me in my tracks. I just stared at him and took a step back because I felt afraid. I have never seen anyone with leprosy, but I am pretty sure that's what it would look like. He had what looked like tumours on his face in different places and his eyes were so sad that I immediately regretted stepping back. He looked into my eyes and face searchingly and so closely, I was a bit shaken to say the least, so I grabbed my husband's arm. I heard my husband gasp a bit and knew he suddenly saw the man as well. The clothes he wore were old, possibly from the sixteenth century. He reminded me of the hunchback character Quasimodo of Notre Dame. He quickly wandered away ahead of us, but no one else reacted to him. It was then that I realised they didn't see him. When I looked back to where he had been, he had gone as quickly as he appeared. Later in the week I would get to see him again.

Next to Saalbach is Zell am See, a stunning little village which we had visited for years and fallen completely in love with. We spent the day visiting with friends we had made there but by the time we decided to leave Zell am See the weather had turned to thunder and lightning. My husband had had a few drinks and with all the driving and travelling, fell asleep, so I drove. Driving at night, on the opposite side of the road to what I am used to, through the dark roads of the Austrian Alps, in the middle of a raging thunderstorm put me on edge to say the least. In series' of violent flashes everything was being lit up and then going completely black. The man we had seen in the village kept coming into my thoughts and I kept thinking of when Brendan and I drove straight through the prehistoric man. I didn't want to meet the Quasimodo man on this dark, stormy road like that. Thank God I made it back to Saalbach just as the thunderstorm was getting stronger. Between the drenching rain, dropping the keys at the hotel door and a panicky feeling of fear I was so grateful when it finally got into the hotel.

The next day the sun came out and I was sitting having a cup of coffee thinking of the night before and how silly I had been. Suddenly there he was again, walking through and around the people in the square, looking totally out of place. I had the chance to really take time to look and appraise the details. Amazed, I just sat and stared. Looking more closely I saw that his clothes looked more like robes. He had one eye lower than the other with bald patches and growths on his head. Again, no one noticed him even when he would get really close to people. When someone did stop, he would look closely into their face. It was fascinating for me to watch him walking around in spirit, interacting with people and no one being aware of his presence. There was also a big part of me that was afraid and did not want him to come back in my direction. When I looked away for a few minutes he vanished. I did not get to see him after that for the rest of the holiday. Even though I did keep an eye out for him and said prayers for him. I was told later that the deceased know that I can see them, that is the reason they approach me, because they need help through my prayers.

When I returned home I decided that I wanted to go for my motorbike test. I've always loved speed; cars, motorcycles, anything fast. I had been learning to ride a motorbike from some of the best riders in the area. Anyone who has learned to ride can tell you, it's not easy at first. Between braking, shifting and working the clutch I had difficulty coordinating the feet and hand manoeuvres. I would end up jump starting at traffic lights, dropping the bike, or worse - just falling off and lying in the road, which for some reason was hysterical to me. Much to my instructors consternation all I could do was lay there and laugh, but I stuck at it. One day I was out for a bike lesson, I was doing about fifty miles-per-hour when the bike went into a strong wobble. The handle bars were shaking so violently that I don't believe even a very strong man could have held onto them. Just as I was starting to lose my grip something lifted me with a great force off the back of the bike. I hit the road hard as the bike slid off ahead of me. I was badly winded and not able to get up off the road, my instructor Colin was behind me on his own bike trying to get to me. He told me later, he had seen my head bounce off the road. He thought I had broken my neck. Before Colin could reach me a red work van came at speed around the corner. Laying in the road, I had just come to stop and I had no time to move out of the way. In a stunning display of fast reflexes the driver managed to miss me and screeched to a halt. Just then Colin came to my side and began helping me up.

"Is that lad alright?" One of the men from the van shouted. He got quite a shock when the helmet came off and my hair came down. It wasn't very common in those days for a girl to be riding motorcycles. I wasn't fit to laugh but damn did I want to!

The helmet was cracked down the back and the visor was off on one side, but my leather bike gear had saved me. My right arm was totally numb and would not move. The man driving the van didn't know why, but something told him to slow down as he rounded that corner. I came very close to being run over. My motorbike was stuck in the hedge so I went back with Colin on his bike. I only had one arm to hold on, but I finally got back to my car and drove home after that. Colin had urged me to go to the hospital but I stubbornly declined. By the time I got home my arm had started to turn colour and the feeling was returning, but no pain. The next day it was completely black with the bone sticking up under the skin. Fascinated, I could push it down and it would come back up but there was still no pain. I had scraped my right leg from hip to ankle and was a bit stiff, but that was all. ~there is no question that I had been looked after during the accident. I seemed to float through it and I came out of it with very little pain. I still don't know what it was that picked me up off the bike or if it was my own error, but I would not want to go through it again. Sliding up a road at speed and lying in the middle of the road, unable to move, is not fun. Shortly after the accident, I passed my motorbike test. It was another example of heavenly protection for me but there would be more to come.

I was still not eating normally and I was sleeping now more and more. I found it very hard to concentrate on anything and I was constantly exhausted. I would literally drag myself out of bed in the morning, but I would still make it to work. When I got home I slept for about two hours then I would clean and do things in the house till about ten at night. I got into such a habit that I didn't want to leave the house. I could control what I was eating, when I had to sleep, and what I was doing. I don't think my husband noticed my condition but that suited me very well. He was focused entirely on work and was very busy. At the time, there was a big part of me that didn't want to be noticed. I saw myself as being fine as long as I could keep this secret. I didn't want my husband or anyone else to see that I had a problem. I had an outward façade of what I thought was perfection, but inside I was completely apathetic, confused, depressed and worried. I just didn't care any more. I was always on edge so it was better for me to be alone as much as possible or so I thought.

It was one of those so called 'normal days' for me when I went out to post the letters for work. It was a short distance from the office, which took me on a walk at the side of the busy main road. The postbox was against a wall, inches from the roadway. I had just dropped the letters into the letterbox when everything slowed down around me. I turned and saw a huge lorry heading towards me and in my mind came the thought, *all you have to do is step back and you won't be here anymore.* This was such a sudden dark thought; to want to leave life in such a way, but I was in such a bad place mentally and physically and so exhausted that for an instant it seemed peaceful. It was then I felt a hand at my back, gently pushing me forward, away from the road, towards the small red postbox. Suddenly the reality of my situation came crashing back in. I grasped the letter slot on the post box and pulled myself tight to the wall just as the lorry went flying past, inches from my back. The wind of it going by sucked me outwards but I held on tight. I chose to live at that moment. Someone had saved me, their strong invisible hands gently pushing me to safety. The feeling of love and warmth I felt in that moment was unmistakable. As I walked back down the road I had a serious reality check. I began to get a fleeting glimpse of my self-worth that I had not felt in a long time, though things would get more difficult before I made up my mind to make a change. It reminds me of the story of Janette.

Janette brought her daughter Melissa for a reading. They had heard about me from a friend and wanted to see if they could get any messages or insight for their own lives. Janette was a nurse for the elderly and she gave up a lot of her time to gently help others. Her brother John had died six months earlier and she was hoping he would come through in the reading. Janette had nursed John in their home in the final months of his life until he lost his battle with cancer. Janette had a detailed reading, but it was more to do with her needing to look after herself and her health. She left disappointed that John had not come through.

When her daughter Melissa arrived into my reading room the energy was very different. Melissa chatted about her uncle John. She missed him but was also glad he was no longer suffering. She was right in the middle of telling me about him when he popped in. I mean it was like he *jumped* in! I had to laugh, it was so unusual to be caught off guard like that. Melissa stopped when I told her he had arrived. She said she felt tingles and warmth around her. I saw John standing at my left side, facing Melissa in his modern, fitted blue suit contrasting against his red hair with a big smile on his face. I told her how he looked and that he had a great smile. As I watched him in that instant my mind was filled with his words, "Tell her I love them." He said. "I'm so thankful for them looking after me. I'm not in pain any more, I'm in an amazing place and there is no need to be sad for me."

Melissa was astonished. She asked for any other signs or messages from him. I was shown the word 'bell'. Not an image but the word itself. It flashed in my mind, dominating my mind's eye for an instant. I thought, *Okay, as always I'll go with what I am shown*. I asked Melissa, "Does a bell mean anything to you and your uncle John?" She started to laugh and cry at the same time and explained to me that when he was sick, she had given him a bell to ring when he needed anything. The bell had been a bit of an issue with John as he did not like being so demanding on the family. They knew he had felt like a burden to them, even though he never was. He only rang it when he really needed help.

Just then John said to me, "Ask about the message Melissa had written about ringing the bell."

Again she was stunned. Her and her mum had bought a wreath that morning for John's grave and the message they had written on it was: 'Remember we love you John and don't forget to ring the bell.'

No one wants to be a burden. We all try so hard to be perfect so we won't be the ones who are in need. We pretend that we are fine when we're not, which creates even more problems as I was doing in my own life. The truth is that we are all in need. All of us need help at different times in life not only from our angels, but also from each other and we should not forget how much we are loved and how much the love we can give is worth.

CHAPTER 5

Saved by Sickness

I was asked to sing at a wedding just outside of Omagh. My brother Garry had also just got married a few days before and I had been loaded up with all the wedding suits to leave at the dry cleaners when I had finished at the gig. It was Saturday, August 15, 1998. Having all my brother's wedding suits to leave in the dry cleaners was a bit of a responsibility as they had to be back for a certain day or they would be charged for them twice. Every Saturday, without exception, my mum or my husband and I would go to Omagh to shop. It just happened that this Saturday, because of the wedding gig, she had stayed home. I phoned and told her I could take her to Omagh and meet up with her later if she would wait for me, but she decided not to go because some of the family where coming to visit her that day.

    The wedding gig went fine and I left to go into the centre of Omagh town at about 2:45. When I got to Omagh and was going to turn at the road to go into the centre of the town, I got this awful wave of exhaustion, like a sickly feeling, and my stomach was in spasm. I decided that the dry cleaners could wait and I drove on a bit, but then I got to thinking about the late fees for the suits and changed my mind. After all, the suits had to be cleaned and returned. I thought I could just do the errand quickly and get it done with. I was going to go in by another route and again, I suddenly got a feeling of being very sick and weak. Finally I just made up my mind to go home.

    I was driving home on the A5 road about five miles outside Omagh, when I met a train of ambulances, police and fire trucks all racing towards the town. When I saw the helicopters whizzing overhead I started to wonder what was going on, but I dismissed it and headed up to my mum's house. After all it was in the middle of the troubles in Northern Ireland and we were used to seeing such things.

When I got home my mother said, "Oh thank God you're alright!"

On the television behind her were horrible pictures of fire and smoke. The location was familiar to me but I couldn't place it. It was then mum said that a bomb had gone off in the centre of Omagh town. It has come to be known as the Omagh bombing. It was a car bomb and the car had been parked just outside the cleaners that I was supposed to deliver the suits to. I stood in shock. My family knew that was where I was going that day and was sure that I had been killed. I know my angels and guides had looked after me that day, even going so far as to make me feel too sick to complete my errand.

It was a terrible time for the people of Omagh and Northern Ireland. So many people lost loved ones. Twenty nine people died and approximately two-hundred and twenty were injured. It was the largest loss of life in a single incident in the troubles in Northern Ireland up to that date. I was stunned to be looking at this event on the television knowing I would had been there in the exact place, at the exact time it had happened.

It was another life affirming revelation. I started to look at my life in a different way from that event, but had a long way to go. I didn't care about going to parties or events my husband and I would get invited to. I really didn't enjoy the feeling of having to go places just because it was expected. It would cause friction between us, but the way I was feeling, I didn't have the energy to be bothered. I wanted things to change but I was so weak. I knew I had to make more of an effort and the fact that I had been spared twice in a short space of time was making me see that I had a lot to live for. I needed to start making some real changes.

Then, one morning shortly after this, I got out of bed and it was like someone had turned on a light in the dark. I sat at the side of the bed looking at myself. My legs and arms were thin, frail sticks. I felt like I had been roused from a deep sleep. It was the first time I realised how thin I had become. I went to the mirror and just stared. I didn't recognise the person I saw looking back at me. My clothes were hanging off of me, I had black circles under my eyes and this emaciated, bony body. I realised for the first time just how dead I felt inside. If someone had said, 'I am going to cut off your arm,' I would have said, 'Yeah sure, that's fine.' I was weary, listless, and had no concern about myself. I didn't care if I lived or died. I wasn't in control of the important aspects of my own life. I had forgot to ask myself in my own life; what did I need, what did I want. I was lost and I felt that everyone else's needs were so much more important than my own. I wanted to feel energised, happy and have worth within myself again. But I was the only one who had the key to give me all those things, no one else could.

There is so much more I could write about my health at this time, but I don't want to dwell on that. Having an eating disorder is a terrible thing to go through. You feel others just won't understand and you feel desperately inadequate in every way possible. It makes you want to not be seen or helped. You feel embarrassed and weak so you want to hide it all. To anyone that is going through this awful illness or any illness, please ask for help.

Your angels will help but you have to take the first steps towards that healing path yourself. Once you choose to heal then it starts to get better. Amazing things happen when you start to love yourself again and see your worth. This story is about the hope, help, love, positive changes and new beginnings that come with the help of the Divine. The awareness of the reality of my situation had suddenly returned and I could finally see what I had done to myself. I just sat and cried.

It was the start of big changes and I wondered how I was going to get the strength to make them. There was so much to think about. My life was centred on my husband and what he had created in the world. That had been norm for me for so long, but I was changing and so was what I wanted in my life. For fourteen years of my life I had managed the accounts of our business. What would I do if I left? I had nowhere to live, no job, and no money. Fear of what would happen surfaced in a big way and not eating or sleeping added to the mental anguish. I realised I would have to start making some sort of plans to change, but my efforts were halfhearted. I suppose in a way I was still hoping that things would change by themselves and I would end up being happier and healthier. Maybe my husband would see how I was feeling and would want to change how things were. I did try to talk to him at different times about how I felt, but I found it so hard. I didn't want him to see me as a weak person, or an insecure person that was creating problems. All I could hear was, "You're imagining things." and, "Don't rock the boat." In the frame of mind I was in I didn't think that change would be welcome. Things had stayed the same way for so long and he did not see anything wrong. I had not even tried to sit him down and explain how I was feeling or what was going on with my health. I just did not have the strength or the courage to.

We had everything that most people would be over the moon about; a beautiful home, cars, holidays, and a thriving business, but I felt so down because of my eating problems. Communication between us was bad and only becoming worse and I was so miserable that it didn't help. I knew I had to make a solid effort and create what I needed in my life. I know now that, yes, we are guided and helped by the Heavenly realms, but we have been given free will and the angels never interfere with this. They cannot make the change for us, we have to step forward and take action to change. At the time I had the tremendous yet emotionless desire to leave where I was and get away. This feeling drove me on. I had no other thought in my mind but to find a place to live. I had never lived on my own and really hadn't given much thought as to what it would be like. I went for drives to see what was available in different areas. I knew I wanted somewhere quiet and a place where people didn't know me. It seems like a simple enough thing, but it was daunting for me to think this way. No one around me was aware of what I was doing, but that didn't faze me at all. My husband didn't notice anything out of the ordinary but I didn't want attention. I think that moving home so much in my childhood actually helped me in this situation.

One Sunday I drove to a place called Dyan. It was about eleven miles from where I lived and the house for rent there was lovely. There were a row of cottages that had just been restored. I stopped and took down the details and the following week I made an appointment to view one of the cottages. When I first stepped in the door I knew that this was where I was going to live. It had been beautifully done up. There was a stove in the sitting room, the rooms where painted in shades of cream and blue with a cozy kitchen and a window that looked into a stone walled yard. The stairs led up to two bedrooms and the bathroom had been decorated with old style fittings. I thought it was just the place for me. Unfortunately the cottage had no furniture, so I had to think of how I would get the pieces I needed. I had the place rented about a month before I decided to leave my home and move in. In the month before I left, I secretly took a table and chairs that had been lying in the garage over to the new place. For months, it was the only furniture I had.

  Earlier I mentioned that the numbers seven and nine were reoccurring in my life. The two numbers seem to come into my life at times of great change. I only started to notice this in my twenties when I got married and left my mother's house. My mum's address numbers are one, nine and seven. The number of the house that I lived in when I got married was number nine. I was so surprised when I learned that the address number for my cottage in Dyan had number nine in it. I only noticed it after I moved in, which was incidentally, on the ninth day of the seventh month in the year two thousand. The house next door had a number seven in it. My husband and I had a number of different properties; the beautiful cottage in Donegal, I call it Pollyanna's Cottage after the name that my father used to call me. The reference for it is one, nine, seven, but I will tell you more about Pollyanna's Cottage later on. When I left the house at Dyan three years after I moved into it, I then moved back in with my mum for a while until I had a beautiful log cabin built. I live there now and the address is again one nine seven. I call the log cabin Angelwood, and like Pollyanna's Cottage, I will tell you more about it later in the book.

Some people call this kind of thing coincidence, but the importance of the numbers seven and nine was made known to me later when I began to write messages from the angels through what some call 'automatic writing'. The number seven is for the seven Archangels of the Lord, and the number nine is to do with my life on earth. When there are recurring signs in our lives we can look at them or ignore them. Every day, the Divine communicates in many ways with you. When you are open to it, it can be truly life altering, giving you the strength and courage to make positive changes for yourself and the world around you.

Now, getting back to the house in Dyan. I moved my clothes over a bit at a time. My clothes were all I would really take with me from the old house. The strange thing was, my husband didn't notice the clothes or that the table and chairs were missing. Uncertain of when I was going to leave, I carried on as usual like the emotionless person I had become. It was easy to go un-noticed. I was glad that I was never asked how I was feeling or what I thought. I felt a great sadness when I thought of leaving and I knew it would not be easy for my husband either. When I did leave it broke my heart, but I knew it was for the best for me. I felt like I was living in such an unhappy way that I just needed to be alone and heal. That's what I needed more than anything else. There are small things you start to notice in a love relationship. There should not be frustration on the face of the person you love when you arrive into their company or see a frown before a smile each time you try to get some time to chat to them. You should not have to stand and wait for their decisions about everything and feel they have the final say from the least important to the most important issues. We are created for love and growth and it cannot be controlled by anyone unless we allow it. Even though we may love someone dearly, it may not be a healthy situation to be in. In those situations we need to really look at what is best for us and our lives. Because we care so much for others we can give ourselves away to them energetically and we lose our true selves, like in this woman's story.

Colette was a tiny lady full of boundless light and energy, and she also did healing and spiritual work. She had been feeling very tired and drained when she arrived in to me. I knew what was happening to her had something to do with her work. It's really important when doing spiritual work to be protected and grounded to keep you healthy. When people come along with all kinds of worries and woes to be helped and healed it can be draining in so many ways if we do not know how to keep it at bay. In my past I had let others take away my energy and had become quite ill because of it and it was now a similar situation for Colette.

She explained to me that she had been feeling fine until about a month before she came to me. She had started to feel depleted of energy when a personal friend of hers had become her client that needed healing. She thought so much of this person that she would literally be on call for them any day or time they required it. Her friend was going through an illness but Colette was not putting up her normal boundaries with this particular person. It can be an easy situation to fall into when doing spiritual work but if it leaves the healer drained then it is better to step away and recommend someone else for them. When the angels and guides arrived they brought her granny with them. Colette had been very close to her granny and missed her so much when she had passed on. She said it felt like she was being hugged and wrapped up in a huge duvet. The feeling of being hugged and secure made Colette very emotional and helped to open her up and she let her tears flow. She apologised for being so emotional, but I understood that it was necessary. She explained how much she had been worrying and caring about her friend's sadness and illness. When she was explaining this part to me I watched as her deceased grandmother started pointing at her neck and a beautiful chain that she had around it. I could just make out the outline of it on her grannies neck and there seemed to be a medal hanging from it. Sometimes the deceased people that come in with the angels can fade and get stronger when I watch them. I was being told by my guides that the necklace was important to Colette and the work that she did. At first I did not know how to explain this to Colette but I only had to say to her, "Your granny is showing me a necklace that is important for you when you do your work." I could not see at this time how her granny showing me a necklace from the spirit realm was going to help Colette on the earth but I waited to hear what she thought.

Colette thought for a bit and then she said, "Oh! When granny died she left me a necklace with a miraculous medal on it, I put it away to always have it and look after it."

I knew this was the medal that her granny was showing me and I told Colette that this chain and medal was to be worn by her or have it in the room with her while she did her work for protection and to help her energy. She was delighted and happy that her granny had come through and had a message to help her with her work. My guides also let her know that her friend needed healing, but to not let the needs and hurts of her friend make her drained and ill. She had to have boundaries, even with her friend. This was especially the case when helping the people she loved most. She had to be careful to not let her protective boundary down just because it was a family member or friend.

It can be the hardest lesson for anyone to not let the people they love drain them or become too dependent on them for too much help. Being a loving and caring person is wonderful, but it is also important to remember it can be costly in certain situations to our health, to our emotions and to the balance in our lives.

Colette said she had felt an amazing release of heaviness lift from her and although she was tired she felt happier than she had for some time. Colette comes back to me now and again and told me that after the first time we met she had improved so much in how she was feeling she could not stop smiling for days afterwards. Her energy improved and also how she was dealing with her friend. She explained to her friend that she was there to be as good a friend as she possibly could be, but that she also needed her to look for another person to do what Colette had been doing. This had improved their relationship and friendship for the better. The angels and guides do so much more for us than we could ever do alone.

A Heavenly Gift

Pauline Johnson

CHAPTER 6
Bats & Beginnings

I left my marriage on the ninth day of the seventh month in the year two thousand. I sat down and I told him I was leaving. It didn't take a lot of time. I knew if I didn't keep going towards the door that I would never leave the house. I got into my car and drove to my new home in Dyan. Little did I know that this small, courageous act was the beginning of a profound change in the way the angels and spirits interacted with me.

Dyan was a very quiet area and just what I needed. No one knew me in the area and that was fine with me. When I arrived at the house it was just nice to go in, lock the door and sit for a bit. I think I was in shock. I found it hard to believe I had left my home only twenty minutes before and I was reeling with emotions. I just wanted to sit and make everything stop. I sat for quite awhile looking out the tiny window at the front of the house. Then my brother Nigel arrived and we chatted for a time. It was good to talk to someone to keep my mind off of the new surroundings. It would take a long time to sort through it all - a new house, a new area, and a new way of living. It was very different from the life I had lived for twenty-five years and I was overwhelmed to say the least. I did my best to make myself comfortable with what I had. The first thing I did was to light a fire in the wee stove. It created a cheery and cozy atmosphere and instantly made the place more homely. I had no bed so I slept on a mattress on the bedroom floor. I did that for about 3 months. I did feel afraid at times being alone and living in a strange area, but also amazed that I had had the strength and drive to take this massive step. I asked myself many times if I was making the right choice, if it would all be ok, and what was I going to do. Of course I was constantly wondering how my husband was feeling and what everyone would think. I knew that I could not heal in a place where I had been feeling ill and that was my old home, so being in Dyan was freeing in a way for me. The first night I tried to settle in, but it was very difficult to get any sleep.

It helped me that at this time that I had a small amount of money. It allowed me to get a few things that where very much needed to make the place more liveable. I was living in the house about three months when I started to feel extreme cold at times. I just put it down to the cold outside, but it seemed to get much worse when I would go to bed. The odd thing was that the only part of the house that was cold was the bedroom. In bed at night I could see my breath, it was like being in a freezer. I told my family and they thought it was that I didn't know how to use the storage heaters, so I decided it must be the heating and carried on as normal.

I booked a holiday to go to Zell am See, Austria for my mother and me, just to get away for a bit. It would be mum's first time in Austria. Because I had friends there I knew it would be fantastic to take a break. It was around my second month living in Dyan and I would go and visit my mum every week and sometimes stay over at her house. It was nice to be able to do that and not feel so alone at times.

The day before our trip to Austria I packed the last things into my case and was going to mum's to stay overnight as we were leaving at five in the morning. My brother Nigel had just left my place and was going up to mum's as well as he was dropping us off at the airport. I was still in contact with my husband and it was his birthday the next day. I had bought him a birthday present and was going to leave it off to him on the way to my mum's that evening. After everything was packed I headed out to my old house.

I was only about three miles from Dyan and I was going around a bad corner when I met an oncoming car on my side of the road moving at speed. I gasped, knowing I had nowhere to go to get out of the way. My steering wheel moved like it was out of my hands and my car was turned left and then right, I had no control. The car coming towards me had shot past me as my car headed across the road and launched through the hedge. In typical fashion, time slowed. My headlights flashed across the trunks of huge oak trees and I closed my eyes as the car rolled in mid-air. At that exact moment I felt strong hands on my shoulders and a strong, male voice speaking close in my ear:

"Relax back into your seat, you will be wrapped up like you're in cotton wool."

This may seem like a strange thing to say since cotton and wool are separate things. But understand that the angels and spirits try to communicate in terms that you, personally, understand. Being wrapped in 'cotton wool' is a saying that I am instantly familiar with. The voice continued:

"When the car stops, you will lift your bag, keys and phone and climb out the driver window."

Then came a loud thud as my car flipped over mid-air and slammed into the earth. The impact was so intense it blew all of the windows out. I felt the shower of glass as I continued to roll another three times. The sound of crunching metal was deafening. The car finally came to rest on its roof and I found myself upside-down, hanging from my seatbelt. Shaken and disoriented I looked out of the small opening where the window had been. I had to shield my eyes from the dazzling beams of lights that surrounded me, lighting up the field. The lights were just confusing for me as I struggled to get out of the car. I undid my seatbelt and, remembering what the voice had told me, lifted my bag, phone and keys and crawled out the window. As I stood up, I was astonished to see about eight men coming towards me. They had been working in the field and had seen the accident. They had these bright torches with them to help them work in the dark. I learned from them that the car had gone about twenty feet into the air and rolled several times. They couldn't believe I was alive and unhurt, but I knew luck had nothing to do with it. My guardian angel and spirit guides had been there with me, keeping me safe through the whole thing. I still remember the feeling of that strong and beautiful, safe embrace as the car flew through the air.

A Heavenly Gift

After the accident I phoned my brother and he came to pick me up. It was about ten o'clock at night when he got there. Looking from the wrecked car and back to me, he couldn't believe that I had climbed out of it in one piece. Still a bit shaken I got to my mother's at last and still managed to leave my husband his birthday present.

While visiting my husband that night, a bat flew in and started doing circles around the sitting room. I thought, *I have lived in this house for nearly fifteen years and never seen a bat*. It seemed to have fallen down the chimney. Then, as quickly as it had appeared it was gone. I learned later that a bat symbolises rebirth, new beginnings, and a need to leave the old and bring in the new. Again, the signs are always there if we know how to look.

When I finally got into bed that night, I started to shake uncontrollably. It must have been delayed shock. It was scary, but there was nothing to do but wait until it went away. While I lay there shaking I turned focus to the strong hands and beautiful voice that had protected me. It was such a clear strong voice. At no time did I question or doubt anything I was hearing, I just sat back in the car and surrendered. In a surreal way, it felt like I had just watched as it all happened.

The following morning we left for Zell am See. As we flew out from Dublin airport I had lots of things going on in my head; the car was wrecked, the insurance had to be sorted, but what was still upmost in my mind was the person or angel that had kept me safe. It had been an incredible twenty-four hours. I had got next to no sleep, the morning had come in a blink and soon we were on our way. My family had wanted me to go to the hospital, but I felt fine the next day. The flight was only two hours and thirty minutes and I slept the whole way.

Zell am See has breath taking scenery. The alps rise up all around the town in steep, snow covered rocky peaks so close it seems like you can touch them. A pristine mountain lake borders the old world town full of quaint shops and wonderful cafés and restaurants. It was so regenerating to be there with my mum. My mother has never questioned or doubted anything I have ever told her about my experiences with the angels or deceased, she has always been supportive and accepting. When I have, at various times in my life, doubted my ability and myself, chatting to my mum always helps. Her wisdom and love picks me up and gives me perspective. She also makes me laugh at my own seriousness and that's great. Of course, it is only through God, the Holy Spirit and His angels that I have any gifts at all. I am always humbly grateful for the gifts I have been given.

As we were in beautiful Austria for two weeks, we booked some trips. I wanted to take mum to so many places, but two trips a week was enough because of the distance we would have to travel. We decided the first week to go to the Grimmal Falls, the highest waterfalls in Europe. The second trip was on the oldest steam train in Europe because my mother loves old trains. The second week came along quickly and we went to the Lichtenstein gorge saving the best for last; a trip to Venice for the day. I had been to Venice before and really wanted mum to see how beautiful it was. The journey to Venice took five hours, though it didn't feel like it. We went through Cortina on the way then hopped on a boat into the ancient city.

There are thousands of people in Venice in the summer months and this was September, so it was still buzzing with activity. The temperature was thirty-five degrees (around ninety-five degrees Fahrenheit) and we had the most beautiful day. We wandered for a while, up and down the tiny streets into the market area and then decided to take a break and have some coffee. It was glorious to just sit and watch the people. After coffee we went back into St. Mark's Square. We wanted to see inside the Basilica but the queues were so long and it was so hot we went on one of the gondolas instead. We were about to take a gondola when an older gentleman came up and said, "No, no, I take you!" He gestured with a flourish at another boat and all the younger gondoliers smiled and backed off. This was the man who ran the whole operation. In dramatic Italian style, he produced a rose for my mother and helped her, red cheeked, into the boat. He was a consummate gentleman and gave us an unforgettable tour of the waterways of Venice. Afterwards we headed back to the bustle of the square, had lunch and sat on the steps to rest. I noticed a man with sunglasses wearing a blue suit and carrying a briefcase. There was nothing unusual about him, apart from the fact that he just stood holding this briefcase, staring in my direction. I tried to ignore him, but he didn't move. I turned to my mother and told her about him she then noticed him too. We decided we had better move to another place in the square, but everywhere we went he was there at a distance. I was getting very scared at this stage. At one point, we thought we'd lost him, but while as I was looking in a shop window I could see him in the glass behind us. I began to get more angry than afraid and I turned from the window to confront him, but he wasn't there. He had just disappeared. I knew there was something strange about this man. It wasn't until later, when I had connected to my angels that I asked about him. I was told that he had lived in Venice and had died just shortly before my arrival. He knew I could see him and he wanted my help. After learning this I felt bad that I had not been brave enough to relax trust my senses and help him. I did pray for him later on.

The deceased people I have seen appear to me as solid, as someone alive, but it is not always like that. There can be a deceased person present and they don't show themselves at all. I can feel them when they are coming through, and know what they are trying to communicate. I actually hear them or see them and sometimes they will show me items. There are no hard, fast rules. That's where the words clairaudient (hearing), clairsentient (feeling), clairvoyant (seeing), claircognizant (knowing), are used to explain a particular gift. I have a bit of all of these things. I will explain further as I go into more about my experiences with the spirit realm.

  We returned home with fond memories and our batteries fully recharged. It had been a needed diversion to be away, but I now had to face arranging a car and making my place in Dyan more of a home. It was a lonely feeling to be going back to Dyan alone. The insurance company judged my car completely wrecked and gave me the use of a car until things got resolved. After making such drastic changes, my life was still as up in the air as my car had been and would be for some time.

A Heavenly Gift

Pauline Johnson

CHAPTER 7
Levitating Letters

Being home again was great, but it also brought the problems crashing into my mind again. They all would have to be faced and dealt with no matter how much I would have liked to run away from all of it. I had to start to think of what I wanted to do and how I was going to organise things. I was working in an office part time it was all I had the energy for. I was also working on making myself healthier and eating better, it would take some time though.

I had stayed at my mother's house the night we got back from Austria, so I arrived back at the house in Dyan the next afternoon. It felt so strange for me to be on my own again after spending two weeks in my mum's company, but I also knew I had chosen to make these changes and I had to get on with things. As soon as I went in the door, I made the decision to start to make the place more homely and comfortable. I slept well that night, thinking of the plans I had made to improve the place. It helped me at the time that I had a small insurance payment coming to me it made it possible to look at buying some furniture. I was tired of sleeping on a mattress on the floor and I was overdue for a real bed. I was also able to buy a suite of furniture and a few more items including a small portable television. It was fine for me and fitted in well in the tiny house. It took about a month to sort everything out, but when it was done it made the place feel cozy. I got back to my love of cooking, so I would cook for my family and have some of them over to visit at different times. I began to look at divorce details and annulment procedures as well as having to sort out an agreement between my husband and myself. I was not aware it would all take so long to bring closure to all of these events, but I had to start.

Even though I was trying to settle in as best I could, I realised it was not a permanent solution. I was thankful to have the house and a place to go without bothering others with my woes, but I knew that eventually I would have to find something more permanent. I again started to notice that the house was getting extremely cold in places again. I had been in the house about five months and I was not sleeping very well at night. I was always restless with strange dreams and would wake up nearly every night thinking I had heard noises.

I got up from one of these restless nights and went into the kitchen to make tea. Glancing at the clock on the dresser, I noticed that it had been turned sideways. I thought that someone must have moved it, I knew it had not been moved by me, but when I passed the other two clocks in the house, they where also turned sideways. I thought it was funny, but just turned them back the right way. I asked my family the next day if anyone had been fooling around with the clocks, and of course, no one had.

Eventually it slipped from my mind until two days later, the same thing happened again. I am sure my family thought I going mad, but the second time it happened I was a bit shaken by it. That same evening, I put the fire on, lit some candles and decided to have a bath and watch a movie. The house felt so peaceful and looked lovely as I sat down to watch the movie. I was only sitting for about fifteen minutes when I saw a movement to my left on the shelf. As I watched, a letter floated up from the shelf all on its own. It levitated all upwards about a foot off the shelf, turned straight up then slowly came back down to where I had left it earlier.

Now I know there are people reading this that are thinking that I should have run screaming from the house, but I just sat there looking at the spot for a few seconds. After all I had been through I thought, I was just trying to have a nice peaceful evening in my new home. I suddenly got very angry and said, "I am watching a film and I am not moving until it is over!" And that is exactly what I did. It had taken so much time, effort, worry and stress to get to this point, I was not letting any object, levitating or not bother me.

When the film ended I went upstairs to the bathroom. I was only gone for a few minutes when I returned to the living room. The television program that had been on was different from the one I had been watching after the movie. I thought, it can't be over that quickly, but the television had been turned to a different channel. I turned it back to what I had been watching, but I wasn't interested anymore. It was a bizarre evening to say the least. I made myself a cup of tea and knew for sure, for the first time, that the house I had rented was haunted. I could not bring myself to stay in the house that night so I stayed at my mums. Telling my mother about the levitating letters, the changed channels on the TV and the turned clocks made it even more real for me. I knew I had at least one spirit in the house, maybe more and that they wanted to let me know in a very real way that they were there. I would know later what they looked like as well. I knew I could always live at my mothers if I wanted to and it was a comforting thought, but I thought I had to sort out my life and not bring my fears and problems to other people. The next day, after a good nights sleep, I drove back to Dyan. Going in the door I knew I was not alone in this cozy mill house. I sat down and said out loud, "I am going to live here and I am not leaving until I decide to, so stop turning over the television and stop moving things around that are not yours." If anyone, and I mean in a real sense, not from the spirit world, had been watching or listening to me I don't know what they would have thought. This new problem caused me a lot of worry and emotional turmoil, but I refused to be put out of a house. I had decided to make it my home. It had taken so long to find the house and to sort it all out I wasn't going to give in without a fight.

Things at the house were quiet for a while after this. I was given a dog, she was a fluffy, beautiful fur ball and I named her Holly. The walled garden in the back on the house was a great place for her. I loved to go on long walks with her and would often go to the local forest parks and walk in the area around Dyan. It made living there feel more normal. Around this time my brother Nigel moved into the house next to mine. It was so great for me to have him around. He was looking for somewhere to live and needed to get a house so it worked out very well. It made me feel safer to have my brother living next door. Nigel had two daughters, Aiobh (pronounced: Eve) and Elle, and then later a boy, named Ronan. They are such wonderful kids and I love them to bits. I think it was more than just a coincidence to be living in houses next to each other. We were both going through similar problems at the same time. It was so nice just to have their wonderful energy next door. With the kids around it brought great joy to me, and to see them so often was really uplifting in so many ways.

Living in Dyan I was always aware that strange things could happen, and I had pushed those fears to the back of my mind. I went to bed as usual and was trying to get to sleep when I started seeing my breath in the air, the extreme cold had returned. My first thoughts were that the heater wasn't working. I got out of bed and switched on the electric heater in the bedroom, but it didn't help to make the room any warmer. I got back into bed anyway, switched off the bedside lamp and was dozing off to sleep when I felt a heavy weight on the left on the bed. Immediately I became more awake, but just at the same time I felt two hands one on each arm, just below the shoulders pinning me down. The hands held me painfully tight and I couldn't move. Then I felt that someone was looking into my face, but my eyes were shut tight. No matter how hard I tried I couldn't get my eyes open to see. I struggled to reach the lamp at the side of the bed, but it was no use. Terrified, I felt perspiration on my face and arms. The air itself was thick with fear. Finally, after what felt like minutes, it stopped. I jumped and switched the lamp on. I had beads of perspiration on my arms and face, but the room was still freezing. I was still the only one in the house. I was drained and totally exhausted and I felt like I had a bad flu coming on. I could still feel the pressure of the hands on my arms. Finally as the temperature in the room returned to normal I stayed up for a bit and then went back to bed, keeping all the lights on.

When I woke up in the morning, I turned to the right in my bed, glad to see daylight through the curtains and there, in full view and as clear as day, was the figure of a man. He had his back to me and seemed to be walking away from the bed. He had shoulder length hair and wore beige trousers and a white shirt with tall boots up to his knee but I never saw his face. As he continued walking away from me, he disappeared. I was in a state of shock and amazement at the same time. Even so, I was not long getting out of the room and down the stairs. Somehow I usually managed to stay calm and be logical when things like this happened, but it was always more than a little disturbing. I don't know why I was not as afraid or as freaked out as I maybe should have been. I guess that I was dealing with so much in my life at this time that I was too frustrated to care. When I told my family what had happened, they thought I was mad to stay in the house. In Nigel's house he had cold spots as well and were mostly upstairs just the same as in my house. He was also starting to hear noises in his house.

One night my niece Gemma, was asked up to babysit for Nigel's kids. No one told her about the things that were happening in my house, Gemma would not have come anywhere near the houses if we had have told her. Nigel, my brother Brendan and I went out for that evening and had a great time. On the drive back we got a call from Gemma telling us that she could hear weird noises in the house. We assured her we would be there soon, but when we arrived Gemma was clearly a bit freaked out. She said she would not babysit again in the house. She had heard children crying and moaning and bangs in the house all evening. It wasn't Nigel's kids they had been fast asleep so it had really scared her. We did tell her later on about the things that had gone on needless to say she was not very happy. Other family members that had stayed overnight at times had very bad nightmares and did not sleep well at all.

It was at this time, through a friend, I was introduced to two beautiful girls that where doing drawings of angels and had angel cards. I found it all totally fascinating because of the things I had already experienced and seen. I was very interested to find out more. I went along and had a wonderful drawing done for me of an angel. This was where I was introduced to angel cards. It was the first time I had seen anything like this. I was told then I could use the cards to read and help others. It wasn't something I had thought about at all, but as I looked at the cards with all the beautiful images of angels I had this feeling of warmth and safety. It felt like coming home. I looked into different sets of cards and what was available and eventually got my own set.

The angel messages that came through at this time from one of the girls made sense of a lot of things that had happened to me and why. The angels explained that I can see the deceased, and about the man I had seen in Venice. I also mentioned earlier in the book about a high-pitched sound I had only heard twice in my life. It is so high it can make a person be a little deaf for a time. This is the angelic realm letting me know they were present around me in my life and are here for all of us on earth, and that they can make themselves known in lots of wonderful ways. I also found out at this time my guardian angel is called Serena. When God's angels are around, there is the most fantastic feeling of lightness and of being wrapped up and loved. Their energy has warmth to it. I was also made aware at this time that darkness in the spiritual realm is very real in the world and there can be dark angels as well, so I always ask for the angels of God's love and light, as we all should if we invite angels into our lives.

CHAPTER 8
Livin' in Dyan

I had been living in Dyan now for about two years and it certainly had its ups and downs. I was still going back and forth between the court and offices to keep things moving forward with my divorce, but the going was slow. Holly, my dog, was much bigger now and full of energy, so I would walk her as much as I could. As much as I needed it, I still struggled to find peace. There were people pulling at me from lots of different places. I had gone to Pollyanna's Cottage in Donegal, for a break with my nieces while their dad, Nigel was on holiday. Aiobh was about four years old and Elle was nine months old at the time

I got up the first morning after a relaxing night at Pollyanna's and my mother called me to come quickly. I went to the window and there was a man taking photos of my house and watching us with binoculars. I thought, *you have to be kidding, the most beautiful scenery is behind you and you are taking pictures of a house that's not even finished?* I knew his intentions were not good. I put on my coat and went straight down to where he had been but he had gone. There were several times after this I was aware of being followed. We came back home with the kids a few days later, but it was not a relaxed break with the thought of some peeping tom about or a person watching me at all.

People living around me in the Dyan area had noticed me living there too. One evening while I was visiting Nigel, there was a knock on his door. When he answered it there was a man asking for me. Nigel said I wasn't available. He told Nigel he had plum trees and berry bushes across the road from the house, growing in the ruins. He said I could pick as much of the fruit as I wanted and he was just stopping by to let me know. It all sounded strange. I had no idea who the man was and why he would come to Nigel's door to leave a message with him that was for me. The next day Nigel went and checked out the ruins where all this fruit was supposed to be. He found no fruit trees or bushes, only the decaying remains of a dead dog. He got a strange feeling about the place and didn't like the ruins at all. It was all very odd to say the least. It was a short while after this incident that I had a knock at my door.

It was about seven in the evening. Normally I would not have answered the door when it got dark unless I knew my family where calling. It just happened that night I was making dinner for some of my family for nine o'clock. I assumed it was them at the door, but it was the same man that had been at Nigel's door about the fruit. He said his car had broken down and asked if I would give him a lift to his house to get some help. I told him that I was too busy and had people coming over to visit. I did mention to him that since he was from that area he might try and ask someone he knew. He said he could not get anyone else at home. I should have told him to go away, but I didn't like leaving a person stranded with no help, so I said I would give him a lift. From the time he got into my car, he sat sideways looking at me silently while I drove. I felt every nerve on end. It took me back to the man giving me a lift years earlier that had the gun under his drivers seat. This man was looking at me in the most intense way. I couldn't wait for him to get out of my car. We were in the dark, on narrow roads that I was unfamiliar with. Eventually I said, "Ok where is this house, I have gone far enough, if we aren't there soon, I'm going back." I was angry and my voice sounded very loud in the quiet in my car. I think that's what snapped him out of the staring mode. Just as I had made my mind up I was going back home, we came to a set of large, dark sheds. For the first time he spoke, "Stop here." He opened the door, turned and leaned towards me in a fast scary way, it was far too close for comfort. It was not kindness I saw in his eyes and then he got out. He never said thank you, or goodbye, not a word. I thought to myself, *Pauline you are such a silly cow to drive in the dark with a man you do not know!* When he finally got out of the car, I locked the doors and turned my car around. The ominous buildings were in complete darkness and he was nowhere to be seen. I knew he was being deceitful and not telling me the truth about breaking down or needing a lift. Where I had let him off looked derelict as well. I thought it would be the last of the fear I would feel from another human while living in Dyan but I was wrong.

After the incident with this man, my dog, Holly would start to howl and bark in the back yard after twelve o'clock. This happened three or four times a week. She had been so quiet before I thought it was because I had spoiled her a bit, so I tried to ignore it. After one of Holly's barking sessions I had gone back to bed, but started to have bad nightmares.

I was partially awake when I heard the most menacing vicious loud, growl in my dark bedroom. I was immediately awake when a face flashed right in front of me out of the darkness. It was the worst image I have ever seen in my life. I saw this face in every detail. It was angry, ferocious and devoid of any emotion but pure hate. I have, like everyone heard stories about the devil, and that is the only thing I can associate with what I saw and heard. I could go into more detail about it, but I do not want to linger on the darkness and how it works to create fear and terror. It shocked me, but only for a few seconds. I do know that there can be attacks and infiltration from the dark side of spirituality, but you must come from a good faithful prayerful place in life to stop this kind of thing happening. It was terrifying, but I strongly believe in the power of prayer giving me protection. I quickly had the lights on in the room and prayed the rosary while gathering up to get out of the house. Some may want to know, why the rosary? I feel protected when I say this prayer and I've prayed it since I was a child. After this, I started to think of moving from Dyan. Life was stressful enough having to sort out money worries and eating problems without all the spiritual activity happening as well. I felt overwhelmed with all of the directions I was being pulled in. I could not stay in the house that night after the terrible experience and made my way to mum's that night once again.

Arriving back to Dyan the next day, I was apprehensive to say the least. I also knew I had to get these houses blessed. As a Catholic we get this done if we have a new house or one that has just been moved into. I asked the parish priest to call in to do blessing and it was arranged that he would do Nigel's home as well. Our local priest was a wonderful man and a good friend to me while all the other things were going on in my life. The day he called was a beautiful sunny day, he came into my house first and everything was peaceful and calm. We then went into Nigel's house. Nigel wasn't there but he had left me the keys. It felt different to my place; it was much colder for one thing. The priest had gone upstairs first, and then came down to finish. We were both standing in the living room and the front door was open. He had just started the blessing when the front door banged with such force that it blew out the blessed candle the priest had in his hand. I jumped with fright. There was not even a breeze outside. He just said, " We will just carry on Pauline and ignore that." He was so calm it made me totally relax as he relit the candle. I was so happy to have got the houses blessed. The houses for a while after this had a great peaceful feeling in them.

A month or two later I noticed that the outside lights at the back of the house were not working, so I asked one of my brothers to change the bulbs. At the same time I became aware that the steel gate into the back yard would often be open in the morning even though it had been closed the evening before. The gate was the size of a normal door and made entirely of steel and it took a bit of force to move it. I would make sure I closed it early in the evening because I did not want to do it when it got dark, but at least three times a week, when Holly woke me with her barking, it would be open.

So it was that in addition to the spirit activity, I now believed that I had some kind of stalker lurking around. I had been in Dyan for nearly three years at this time and I was more determined than ever to move. It was about two months before I left that I decided I would sort out the lights at the back of the house. The light coverings were the type that I had to screw the front off to change the bulb, but when I took the glass cover off, the light bulbs had been screwed out of the sockets and left inside the glass. It was the same on all three outside lights. Additionally, the fuse box switch for the outside lights had been turned off in the outside store. I had no key to lock the outside store so it was always open. I replaced the light bulbs and put the switch back on so all the lights were working. The fact that someone had spent time deliberately doing this was extremely worrying for me. It was obviously to do more harm to me than good. I just knew I had to get away and be somewhere I felt safe, so I started to pack things up that evening. I also stayed again at my mums that night. The next day, I made arrangements to leave Holly with my husband. My old home had a lot of room with a big garden but my mum's had no room for her. It was the last time I would have Holly as my dog it made me so sad that I had to give her away. I loved her so much, but I was not in a good position to look after her. I then started making arrangements to move out. It was another few weeks before I left completely to live in my mum's house.

During one of the last weeks I stayed in Dyan, I got up on one morning, came down the stairs and glanced to my left. What was normally there vanished, and was replaced with the image of a man, sitting with his back to me, writing at a desk. He was balding on top and wore a coat with tails and grey, pinstriped trousers. The vision only lasted for a few seconds and then vanished, leaving everything back to normal. I was surprised, but not afraid. I was now used to the unusual happenings in the house. It would be the last spiritual vision I would see in Dyan. I thought of the turned clocks in the house and it came to me that the deceased in the house did not want to see that time had moved on. It was the only reason I could come up with about why they would move the clocks in particular. The spirits I had seen were all dressed in eighteenth century fashion. I was never harmed by any of the deceased in the house, but I had been amazed by what I had seen and heard including the rattling of door handles and the unexplained noises on top of everything else. As the day arrived to leave Dyan, I packed up all my things with a light heart. I was not sorry to be leaving even though I was moving again and it seemed that I was going back to the beginning.

A Heavenly Gift

Pauline Johnson

CHAPTER 9
Back to the Beginning

Back to the beginning, that is exactly what it felt like. I was moving back into my mother's house though I knew it wasn't permanent. I had been away from my mum's for sixteen years, but it was wonderful to have her company and finally feel safe. She always told me to move back any time I wanted, so it was a good time to leave the Dyan area. The things that had started to happen outside the house made it more urgent to move on from there. It was certainly not a safe place to be on my own. I stored most of my furniture in my brother's house. I was happy to be able to relax and had a great night's sleep for the first time in ages. It was wonderful to get up in the morning and have my mum to chat to. I had a lot going on as usual in my mind, but at least I could switch off the worries about the spiritual events, or so I thought.

I was doing psychic work for my family and some friends. Details would come out about things going on around them and it would help them to handle worries and give them hope. I understood that people would be skeptical about what I was doing. I was my own worst critic for a long time. I did not understand how or why I could do this. I am not any different to any one else and 'psychic' is a word that I actually had to look up. Words like psychic, fortune-teller, and the like, are words that conjure up images of crystal balls and séances. To me these words make it all seem dramatic and fear-based. The media in the world doesn't really help either. I do what I do to help and heal other people. I see myself of more of a messenger than anything else. The fact that there can be some cards involved is to me, a minor detail. The cards are used for people to focus, nothing more. I believe in God, Jesus, the Holy Spirit and prayer, and that we are given help every day from Heaven and through our guardian angel as we are told. That is where my guidance comes from. Connecting needs to happen from a pure, enlightened, empowering, Heavenly source and what is said needs to be from the same. Anything else should be questioned. I also pray to be protected and for everyone I read for to be protected as well. I was surprised and hurt at times from the reaction I would receive from people close to me. I have had horrible things said about me and to me, but I also understood that people close to me had not ever known about this part of who I am, I didn't even know until later in my life. I was surprised at the turn my life took, but I was aware it was a very strong part of me and was not going to go away.

I had been thinking of going to a councillor at this time. I had never thought of doing this at any other time in my life. It was daunting for me to even think about, so much had gone on that I had never discussed with anyone. I got the name of a councillor from Belfast. I thought, *if I am going to do this, I don't want it to be someone local.* I made the appointment and headed off to meet him. His type of counselling is to help people see and feel their self-worth, and appreciate themselves enough again to be self-reliant. It was completely out of my comfort zone, but the last three years had strengthened me quite a bit. It does take a certain amount of strength to admit you need help. But it should be as normal as going to get your hair done, or the dentist. We all need help in every area of our lives including, mental and emotional help.

I was nervous but excited. I didn't know Belfast very well to drive in and I was really anxious about getting lost so of course, that is exactly what happened. My appointment was for one o'clock and I arrived in Belfast at twelve, thinking I had loads of time. I drove for most of the hour but had no idea where I was or how to get to the correct part of Belfast. There was no satellite navigation at this time. I sat in a queue of traffic at a set of traffic lights, panicking about not making my first appointment, but there was nothing I could do. I had practically given up when I got a knock on my driver's side window from a man on a motorbike. I hadn't even seen him pull up along side me. I looked at him for a second, confused, then put my window down just a little. I was skeptical of other people approaching me in Belfast to say the least. He didn't lift the visor on his helmet so I could only hear his voice. It was what he said to me next that, I think, made my mouth fall open.

He said, "You are looking for directions?"

I was shocked and nodded, "Yes, the Malone road."

"Follow me." Was all he said.

I hesitated for a second, but then trusted my intuition. He took me straight to the Malone road, and then without me having told him, drove me right to the road to the councillor's house. I stopped, still stunned, and waved. He just turned around, waved and drove on. I never saw his face or got to thank him. I do know heavenly help and communication can come in all guises and ways but this was unbelievable. Another point to this story was particularly interesting to me. As I am into motorbikes, I found it easy to see something in common with this person that stopped to help me. I trusted a biker where I might not trust a motorist. Divine guidance arrives and appears in many different ways, to our amusement a lot of the time.

I got to Fergus's door and it was already after one o'clock so I apologised for being late, but Fergus explained that a lot of people find it hard to get to his house first time around, so when he makes an appointment with a new person he books two hours. Still nervous about the session I had no escape to get out of this meeting so in I went. It turned out to be a wonderful first hour. I would continue seeing Fergus on and off for a year. It helped me in a tremendous way and we are still friends today. We all need help at different times and one thing I have learned in what I have gone through, there is no weakness or shame in asking for help for all kinds of things that can happen in our lives.

Living at my mum's was so different from living alone in Dyan. Her house always had our family going in and out. It was always great to spend time together and have a laugh. I still wanted to be working and I had my own computer and wondered what I would do. I had my spiritual work, but I needed to make a living as well. I went to bed as usual one night, falling asleep thinking about work. Just as I was falling asleep I heard a beautiful voice speaking to me, it said one word, "Photography." In the morning, I woke full of thoughts of photography. It was strange because I had just started to buy magazines on photography. I went and got some more and looked into it in more detail. I read about different types of photography work and what was needed. After some time studying the different aspects, I decided to purchase a camera. It was a professional camera and took the most amazing photos, so I started shooting. I signed up for a course in photography in a town about twelve miles from where I live. I still do photography to this day; mostly landscapes and anything else that catches my eye. I called my photography business 'Mystical Images'. In the course of taking photographs some of the photos reveal some very unusual things. At the time I am writing this I am hoping that I will be able to put some of them in a book and share them with you.

I really enjoy going out and taking landscape photos. We have such beauty all around us in nature and most of the time we take it for granted. I would take the photos back home, work on them and then get them framed. Being in nature has a wonderful healing effect. It has always worked wonders for me, even strolling around a garden centre is uplifting. It can help anyone, just to go outside somewhere quiet, be still and listen. If you have a garden at home it is so healing to just take time in it and appreciate the beauty it holds. I am also a great believer in the healing effects of the sea and water in general. Having a sea salt bath is a great home solution for clearing and relaxing the mind and body. I was doing more of these things when I went back to live at my mums. It was just what I needed to slow me down and see what to do next.

I was still getting messages from the Angelic realms at different times. They explained certain things to me that I could not understand about myself. The angels explained why I had been feeling so tired and that I would know when someone from spirit was around me and how it would feel for me. Doing spiritual work can be draining if you do not protect yourself. As I have said, I use prayer - mainly because this is what I grew up with and I believe protects me. This was all going on when I began to live at my mum's. I was getting all this information, but it was very needed guidance to help me cope.

A Heavenly Gift

One day I was in my bedroom working on some photos at my computer as usual. I had been getting a pain on each side of my head occasionally and it could be quite strong at times. When I would experience this, I always felt that someone was there beside me or in front of me, but there was never anyone in a physical sense. My angels told me that this is how I would feel the presence of the spirit realm. This particular day, I felt a pain on the right side of my head, only this time it was accompanied by a tap on my shoulder. I have to explain that when I work, I can get very engrossed in what I am doing. I thought I had imagined it, but it happened again. I stopped and looked around. I was the only one in the room, but then I heard a male voice. When I say I can hear people in the spirit realm, it is like a voice from outside of me but also in my mind. This man introduced himself as Jack. I stood up at this stage and thought, what is this now? I heard this man saying to me, "I want you to go down to your brothers office." It was very clear and loud. If anyone had of been watching me they would have thought I had completely lost the plot. So I said, "What? Why do I have to go there?" He repeated what he had said the first time. I sat back down at my computer and again asked why. He told me that he had a message for a person in my brother's office and I had to go down and deliver it. Well, it was one thing doing spiritual work for my family and having occasional interactions with spirits, but to walk into my brother's office and give a complete stranger a message was a different thing altogether. I never had a spirit ever demand anything from me before. I thought, *no way*! Then obstinately sat, thinking of all the worst scenarios. Then I said, "How do you know there is anyone there?" I certainly didn't know, but my curiosity got the best of me and I had to go and look if anyone was at the office. Sure enough, there was someone there. I thought, *Oh God, what do I do now?*

Well, Jack was persistent. He was still there saying, "I have a message and you have to deliver it."

Finally, I decided to do it or I would be listening to Jack for hours. I couldn't think of an excuse to go into the office, so Jack said, "Make tea."

Make tea?! I have spirits talking to me and the best they can come up with is 'make tea?' It was so funny I could do nothing else but laugh. Jack has to be Irish, I thought. Tea is the Irish cure for everything. I went and set the tray for tea and headed down to my brother's office. I walked into the office and found my brother Garry, my nephew Darren, and two ladies from the accountant's office. Garry was all smiles and surprised that I had brought tea. I left the tray down and was introduced to the two ladies as Garry's sister. I said hello and then asked if any of the two women knew a man named Jack.

They asked me for more information; where is he from, where does he work, what is his surname? I said, "Oh, this man is dead, I like to say deceased." Garry and my nephew went completely pale. I was amused at the faces but also quite nervous, but carried on anyway; I was getting help from Jack as well. I soon realised which lady the message was for and asked her if I could speak to her in private. Once we were alone I explained to her that I do spiritual and psychic work and that I had a message for her from Jack. When I had asked her before, she had said she was not sure if she knew anyone called Jack, but as soon as she was on her own she told me that she had a friend called

Jack that had died a few years earlier. She seemed quite shaken about hearing from him this way. Jacks message to her was that she had to go straight away and get her health looked at and that if she did not, by September it would be much worse and very serious. I could see the shock on her face. No one else around her knew that she had been feeling unwell. This lady had the early signs of cancer. She was so happy and a little bemused to say the least that Jack, her deceased friend that she had loved so much, had come back to help her and give her that push to look after herself. She was also given a message which was the second shock from all her five children that she had lost through miscarriages that they loved her and they they where happy. But her health was the most important area in her life to get checked right away. It made me realise very strongly right at that moment, that I was just the feet and the voice that Jack needed to help his friend and that it was such a privilege for me to be asked to do it. I had given Jack such a hard time because I was thinking about myself, and what would be thought of me. In reality, it is not important what others think. It is important that I constantly put myself aside and deliver all the healing, and help I can when I am called to do it and that is what I continue to do now. Jack thanked me and I thanked him for being patient, then he left. This is how the spirit realm helps us here on earth. It may be a deceased family member, a friend or an angel of Heaven. It is always different and always filled with goodness and beauty.

Shortly thereafter, I was introduced to one of my spirit guides, called Merlin. I had been hearing this name repeatedly but I had no idea who it was. I could not hear it clearly enough at the start, it sounded like Marvin, or Mervin. I thought this was another spirit looking for help from me. It happened that I could hear his name in the mornings and again before I would sleep. It was like my name was being called and he would introduce himself. It eventually became clear that his name was Merlin. He came into my life shortly after the event with Jack, but this was different. I was receiving wonderful angelic messages to help me and they explained that Merlin was with me from the spirit realm to guide and help me. I did have a laugh when I heard this name. The only time I had heard this name before was in reference to the King Arthur myths, obviously this was a different Merlin. It turns out the name was common in the twelfth century. Even though it was truly incredible to have all of these things happening around me I questioned everything. The angels and guides have serious patience to be dealing with me, I can be so full of doubts at times, but I have had to learn to accept what I do. Merlin would be with me for years, helping to protect me and guide me, later that would change. To describe him, I would have to say he was not unlike a knight of old. He brings the most beautiful light and energy with him when he arrives. The light that surrounds him is truly incredible, brighter that any earthly light I have ever seen. This was to be the start of my introduction to lots of help from Heaven. I was guided to do a drawing of Merlin shortly after this and also later on to do drawings of my other angels and guides.

A Heavenly Gift

Pauline Johnson

CHAPTER 10
Eyes & Ears

One night I went to bed as usual, I had just finished saying my prayers and then decided to read for a bit. I started to feel tired so I turned off the light. What I saw after the light went off is difficult to describe only that it was so immensely beautiful. The angel appeared before my bed, green light pouring off of him, like waves on the sea. He wore long flowing robes of green and what looked like a crown, but it was also like an amazing bright light around his head. I had never seen or experienced anything like it. He filled the room with these waves of green light. Wisps of energy fanned away from him like smoke in a breeze.

There is nothing on earth that can communicate how wonderful it was. Then I heard, "I am Archangel Raphael." And he disappeared. I sat up in the dark and stillness with the most incredible feeling of peace. An Archangel! I did not see wings, just light. It was an amazing vision to behold. I then fell back into a deep sleep. The next morning my thoughts were filled with all that I had seen, it was quite overwhelming. I did know about Archangel Raphael, but now I wanted to know more. I found that Archangel Raphael means, "God Heals", or "It is God who heals." Archangel Raphael appears in the book of Tobit. He first appears disguised in human form as a travelling companion for Tobit's son. He calls himself Azarias, but later makes himself known as the Archangel Raphael, one of the seven who stand before the Lord. In this story, it tells of him healing people. This is why he is known as the Archangel of healing. He is also venerated and patronised as Saint Raphael the Archangel. He is patron saint of medical workers, the blind, nurses and traveler's. His feast day is September twenty-ninth.

A Heavenly Gift

I had always wanted to see an angel, but when it happened it was more incredible than I could have imagined and was such a gift to me. I don't think anyone could prepare for such an experience. I can remember it as clearly now as when it happened and it will stay with me the rest of my life. I have no idea why Archangel Raphael appeared when he did but he left me with a wonderful feeling of contentment and lightness, but I know he is there to call on when I need his help to heal and help others. This was not the only vision I was to see.

I was much more content and happy in my mum's house. It was relaxed, safe and quiet. As much as I enjoyed being there, I knew I had to start to look for my own place. I did not want a massive house or to live somewhere too remote. I was looking through the yellow pages business directory for a number when the thought of a log cabin came into my mind. There was no provocation for the thought, it was just there, strong in my mind. I looked up log cabins in the telephone book and found Wildwood Log

Cabins. I kept the number and decided I would call them later.

Around this time my mobile phone started ringing at strange times of the day and night. This went on for about a week. Every time I would answer it or look who had called, there was no number and no one would speak. I didn't think much of it all until I was left a message on the phone. It was a male voice saying, "Violet where are you? I can't get to you, help me Violet!" It sounded like an old gramophone or an old black and white movie. I thought, *why cant this poor man get to this woman?* I checked the number but it came up blank. I thought it was strange but put it out of my mind. The next day, I had another message. The same voice said, "Violet I am trying to get to you, this is Norman, Violet can you hear me?" Again it sounded like an old gramophone. I listened to the message again, but while I was listening, I was getting a picture in my mind of an English sailor. I had no explanation for the messages on the phone and I was trying to put it together. I had an instinctive feeling I would soon know why I was getting these messages.

A Heavenly Gift

It became clearer when I received a message from the angels. Norman was being put in contact with me to help him. Violet was his wife and she had passed away before him and he wanted to get back to her. Norman had now also died and was asking for help through prayer and I was there to do just that. He had been a sailor and that was why I had seen that image in my head when I listened to the message. I was more than happy to help Norman in a prayerful way, his voice sounded so sad. I do not know why my mobile phone was used for me to receive this message. It made me laugh to think of modern technology being used to convey a message from the spirit realm. This is how it is with spiritual things. The most unusual things happen and sometimes there is no explanation. The only thing that made me think this particular situation was different was the distinct sound of an old gramophone. I prayed for Norman and Violet and I know that in my heart they are together now, it is a beautiful blessed thought.

I was taking time to do my photography and psychic work and going out the odd day on my motorbike, but I still wanted to find a place of my own. Wildwood Log

Cabins came back to my mind, so I rang and spoke to a man named Dean. He was a lovely person and I made an appointment to go and view a log cabin he was working on. The work site was in the middle of a private estate amongst tall beautiful trees at the side of a lake. It had window boxes of flowers and the floor plan was perfect, I just fell in love with it. I knew this was the house for me.

My mum gave me a great piece of ground next to her house to build on. It was a small bit of field that we used to play in as children. The well that I saved Nigel from is at the corner of the property. I remember when I was around about eight years old I used to lay on the grass on this piece of ground and stare up at the clouds worrying about all the things I would have to do when I got older like, learning to drive, passing my exams and getting married. How wonderful and strange it had turned out that it was here that I was to build my cabin. It was exciting for me to start another new chapter in my life with a new house. I ordered the cabin and began preparation for pouring the foundation. The other elements of my life that had to be sorted out were moving much slower. Getting my annulment resolved, along with money problems just made each week drag along. There were always things needed to keep it all moving forward. It was a drain to get up every day, knowing these things where all still hanging over my head.

It would take four months to have the cabin ready to move into. I was still staying with my mum. It was wonderful, and we enjoyed having the time together. I would go out occasionally with my family in the evening and it would be fun but I was not at all interested in meeting anyone for a relationship. I was happy to be alone and was sleeping well for the first time in years.

One night I went to bed as usual and fell asleep. Shortly after I fell asleep, I started to dream. Actually, it was more of a nightmare. I could see a dark hooded figure coming towards me. He was large and very tall and his clothes where like black trailing rags. I could smell the rank scent of sulphur and decay. The smell was so overpowering it made me nauseous. This figure came and stood at the side of my bed. I felt so small, and everything in the dream was dark and frightening. Then he leaned towards me and touched my arm and it was so painful. I could feel myself trying to move in the bed, but I was weak and heavy. I remember calling out to Archangel Michael to help me. Then I was lifted up from my bed, from the middle of my back, and thrown back down like a rag doll. All at once a tremendous light blazed out, cutting through the darkness and Archangel Michael appeared. He was magnificent. I immediately knew who he was. He opened a door and I could see the sun and blue sky as the dark figure evaporated into nothing. Archangel Michael asked me to take a deep breath in and out. I thought I was dreaming but it was all so real, I breathed out and released, what looked like, small seeds with my breath. They went out the door into the sun and floated away. When I woke the next morning, I knew what had happened was real. I had aches and pains all over my body and bruise marks in the shape of a handprint on my arm where the dark figure had touched my arm. I was totally depleted of energy and was exhausted for two weeks after. The angels later explained that I had been spiritually attacked by evil, but knew to invite Archangel Michael in to help me. Nothing else would have been strong enough to drive this from me.

I have seen Archangel Michael twice in my life. This was the first time I had the gift of his presence. Archangel Michael means, "Who is like to God." In the Bible he is called The Great Prince and is usually shown with a sword or carrying the Scales of Justice. Pictures show him wearing armour and slaying a dragon. These are symbols of his strength, courage, truth and integrity. Archangel Michael is engaged in an endless war against the forces of evil. Most people know the image of him casting Lucifer and his followers out of Heaven. In the old testament of Abraham, Archangel Michael told Abraham he was about to die, so Archangel Michael, also known as Saint Michael, has been known for guiding departed souls to Heaven. Joan of Arc began hearing, and later, seeing Archangel Michael from the age of thirteen. The prayer to Saint Michael that I use every day and night protects and helps me each day:

The Prayer to Saint Michael

Saint Michael the Archangel, defend us in battle.
Be our protection against the wickedness
And snares of the devil.
May God rebuke him, we humbly pray;
And do Thou, O Prince of the Heavenly Host-
By the Divine Power of God-
Cast into hell, Satan and all the evil spirits,
Who roam throughout the world
Seeking the ruin of souls.
Amen.

When I saw Archangel Michael, he was surrounded by incredible light. I have read about the colour blue being associated with him, but I only saw a great white light surrounding him. He looked so incredibly powerful it was a beautiful vision of strength. I was to have another vision of Archangel Michael later, though this one would be much clearer.

Even though I had been saved and helped by Archangel Michael, I was tired for quite a while after the attack and it took a while to regain my strength. It felt similar to recovering from a bad flu. I ended up with a bad chest infection and a cough that would keep me awake at night. It took two weeks to finally clear up. I was exhausted, but this is what can happen with spiritual work, it can leave a person very drained and sometimes ill. Even though these kinds of attacks can be very unnerving, I also realise the wonderful gift we have to be able to call on help from Heaven. These attacks can happen in many ways. The darkness can work through the people who are familiar to you, like friends and family. It can be extremely powerful and come in the form of verbal or even physical attacks by people that you love, but it is important to remember that you love them and to always pray for help. It's not them *per se*, it is the darkness working through them. Love always wins, no matter what.

The most beautiful vision I have ever been shown was of Our Lady. The Blessed Mary is the Mother of God, the Mother of Jesus and wife of St Joseph. Archangel Gabriel announced to her that she would become the Mother of Jesus by the Holy Spirit. The feast day of Our Lady is on the fifteenth of August. Mary, the Mother of God is ever present and helps us every day of our lives. Our Lady is also known as the Queen of the Angels, Queen of peace, Mary Queen of Heaven, Star of the Sea and many more beautiful titles. There have been many accounts, rigorously proven, of appearances of the Holy Virgin Mary. Monuments to these powerful heavenly visitations can be seen all over the world at such places as: Our Lady of Lourdes France, Our Lady of Fatima Portugal, and of course the Basilica of Our Lady, Queen of Ireland in Knock, Ireland.

When I saw the vision of Our Lady I could not, and did not, want to take my eyes from what I was seeing. I saw thousands of people, all of them in white robes, all looking up at Our Lady. Her robes and crown were gold and words fail utterly when trying to describe her beauty.

Glory, majesty, magnificence are words that come to mind, but fall short compared to what I witnessed. Surrounding her was a wall of golden angels of all sizes and shapes, some like little cherubs, some tall with enormous wings. The wall of angels was vast, what looked like thousands and thousands of them, but it was Our Lady in the middle that was the most splendid of all. This vision left me feeling serene, blissful and so content. I have no idea why I was given this gift to witness such heavenly beauty, but I'm overwhelmingly grateful that I was. I will never forget it. It happened while I was staying in my mother's house. I had gone to bed, but I was not asleep, I remember every detail of the amazing spectacle and I have not seen a vision as Divinely beautiful as this one since that night.

When these things would happen I would chat about them with my mother, but not to anyone else. I never had the thought that I needed to go and tell everyone. I kept to myself, living a very quiet life and I really enjoyed that. I wanted only peace in my life free of turmoil and strife. I was getting on with the business of building my new home and it was going up quickly. When the construction phase was finished I was so excited. There was a lot of work to still be done before I could move in so I got to work sanding and staining floors, painting walls and cleaning windows. I would fall into bed at night and sleep well, exhausted from the busy days. It was the end of 2003 and I was not going to move into the cabin until the New Year.

I was still going back and forth to court in Belfast to sort out divorce details. The annulment called for the same details to be repeated again and again at different times. I then had to go to the Bishop's house in Dublin to give a statement. It was almost starting to feel normal to be doing these things. I realise now why so many Catholics find it hard to think of getting an annulment. The process is long, drawn out and completely draining, but it is also important and freeing.

Working on my house helped me to feel like I had some sort of a normal life ahead. I needed a break so I booked a trip to Austria again in the New Year for a week's holiday in March. A week in the snow is always great fun and now I had that to look forward to. Christmas was also coming up and there was a lot to feel blessed about. That Christmas, Mum and I were invited to my brother house. Christmas is my favourite time of year. It is such a magical time. Heaven will always send us all such peace and love at this time of the year, but for some people it can be a lonely time. It's especially difficult for those who are missing loved ones that have passed on. It's easy to become melancholy during the holidays. To me, loved ones have just gone through a door to a beautiful place. They have no pain, no illness, just happiness and bliss. It is the people left behind that find it the hardest to move forward. It is understandable to miss your loved ones when they pass on, but they are always there. If people just realised how close they are! When I am doing psychic work and a person's deceased relations arrive, it is the most wonderful gift. It never ceases to astonish me when it happens.

This particular Christmas I was given a delightful gift. I was shown a beautiful vision of cherubs smiling at me and playing around a fountain. They were so childlike and beautiful, but vanished as quickly as they had appeared. It always makes me smile when I think of them.

Even though the past year had been very difficult, the vision of the cherubs gave me hope for the upcoming year.

CHAPTER 11
Challenges & Courage

The start of 2004 was relaxed and settled. I was looking forward to going to Austria again and hitting the slopes. I had been going skiing for twenty years and still love it. The feeling of the fresh air, the snow and being active outdoors is such an attraction for me. Some of the friends I had met there on previous holidays were coming to meet up around the same time. The cabin was coming along nicely with the painting mostly done and the floors finished. It was a blessing to have my own place nearly ready. It wasn't a massive house but it was fine for me. I had some basic kitchen units installed until I could put in a proper kitchen, but I was very happy with the way it was all coming together. I moved into the cabin in February 2004. Staying with mum had been great and the fact that we live just beside each other now is lovely, I just dander around the corner to have a chat.

I arrived in Zell am See on a Saturday evening. I got my stuff packed away and headed out to find everyone else in the local bar and restaurant called the Crazy Daisy where we always gathered to see Sven and Willy and the Daisy mob. It was so great to see everyone together and it was so wonderful to be in each other's company again. It seemed like such a long time since we had all been in Zell at the same time. Over the years, there were always people missing for one reason or another, but this year was different. It also happened that my ex-husband was there at the same time. I did not expect him to be there and I was not sure how the week would go for him or me. We both always enjoyed our holidays so it would be fine. Everyone knew we weren't together anymore and I did hoped it wouldn't be awkward for people. I was determined to have a good time anyway. I did know it would not be any easier for him that I was there either. There were about fifteen in the group so there would be plenty of people around all the time to chat with. One of my friends was Ian, he was a wonderful man for gathering people to him. Ian was about sixty-five years old but he could talk to anyone, no matter what their age and become friends quickly. I had known Ian, Lavinia, his wife and his son Brent for twenty years. It was during this week that Ian met a lovely young couple from England who were on honeymoon and they ended up going skiing with us. I did not know the couple at all and was introduced to them in a funny way. We had agreed to get together at a place called Patrick's Bar for a bite to eat. When I arrived, Ian was explaining about the Irish people having healing hands. Though I watched in amusement, I tried to stay out of it. Ian, of course, asked me to join them because I was the token Irish person. I really had no idea what he was talking about, but I went over anyway.

  As we finished our introductions, I became aware that I had to get the woman to put the palm of her hand under mine. When she did, I felt as if our hands were being pulled together. The sensation was strong, but suddenly it broke and her hand fell away. As I looked at her, information came flooding in. I was told to tell her that she had a very weak lower back and that she needed to rest for at least two days and not try to keep up with her husband. Her back needed to be looked at when she returned home and not to procrastinate going for a checkup any longer. She looked at me completely shocked, but there was more to tell her, I had to remind her that she was on a holiday and she did not need to be making the beds every day in the room and to relax and enjoy her holiday. Her back problems came from her thinking she was inadequate compared to her husband. He was a physicist and his new wife had been feeling this way for a while. The husband was totally unaware of how she felt. They were a wonderful couple and I told her that though her husband was a physics genius, he did not have her gifts that brought so much beauty into their lives. They balanced each other so well, but her husband needed to take the time to notice all the things she did for him. Her husband smiled at me and said that only that morning he had told her to stop cleaning the room and enjoy herself.

She was still a bit shocked. "How do you know about my back problems? And, how do you know I been making the beds and doing all those things since I got here? I've never said a word to anyone about my feelings of inadequacy around my husband." Her next comment surprised me and made me laugh. She said, "You are a witch!"

Well, what could I say to that? I just said, "No, I am just guided to help others if I can." Secretly I thought to myself, *Oh God maybe I look like one*! Not a good look. I thought, *I really must lighten my hair colour.*

We all met up in the Crazy Daisy as usual, and I could sense that I was being looked at a little differently. It was Brent, Ian's son, who broke the ice and asked how I knew all those details about two strangers. I explained about my gifts, that I was given guidance from my angels and spirit guides to help others. I told him that it wasn't me, I was just the messenger, all of which Brent accepted openly and even enthusiastically. My husband, who had known me most of my life, was the next to ask the same thing. I told him, "I only know what the angels tell me" and that was all I said. I was sad when I said that. He would have never been interested in anything about me to do with spiritual work, so I thought, why would I explain it all now?

When this kind of thing happens and I am told to relay a message, it can be stressful. But I still go ahead and deliver whatever needs to be said. I try to do it in a relaxed, calm way. It's usually very shocking for someone to be told things of a personal nature by someone they don't even know. I have received mixed reactions, but I try to not dwell on the negative ones. It is not necessary to have cards or anything else, the messages will come through anyway and it can happen anywhere, just like it did that day on the mountain at Zell am See.

The week in Zell was wonderful, but I had to get back to Ireland to move into my new home. I arrived back home tired from the holiday, but was also excited to be moving on and starting a new phase in my life. I got to work on the move the following day. The cabin was so easy to make cozy and welcoming. I lit the stove for the first time that evening and the warmth filled the cabin as I relaxed on the sofa. The first night was complete joy and I had a great night's sleep. To wake the next day in my own house was incredible for me. It was peaceful, safe and beautiful. It made me giddy to have my own place and do my own thing. I had to paint more doors, windows and walls, but I didn't mind doing it. It was so much fun and the peace I had was surreal. People say that their home is their castle, and home is where the heart is. I truly believe this. Home should be the place that is a haven from the outside world, a sanctuary where you feel happiest and most loved, balanced and grounded.

I continued doing my spiritual work for my family and friends. Doing spiritual work can bring along a lot of dramatic change in life. The growth and change can be so quick that it causes confrontations with people around you, but also self-reflection. Change is a huge part of living and if you struggle with it, life can get extremely hard. My life had changed in a considerable way, but if I had really understood how much help was available to me from God's angels, I would have been more trusting and relaxed. Heaven's help can come from others put on our path to help us, or even from unusual events, but when it does it usually comes in the form of change. After we struggle through the changes, we see that they were really for the best and it becomes easier to accept change as a part of normal living. When we have sudden shocks and trials that create life changing events, it's difficult to resist being negative. We all go through changes one way or another, knowing that you can call on your guardian angel to help you is a comfort and an incredible blessing. God gave all of us this help, and all we need do is invite the angels of God's love and light into our lives. I can say from doing spiritual work for so many people that we all share common problems and worries. Things happen that seem dark and sad and that take tremendous strength and energy to face like the death of a loved one, divorce, health problems and money worries. Many of these things then cause, worry, guilt, depression, low self-esteem, jealousy, sadness, aggression and stress. It all happens when change and fear come into our lives. I have dealt with some of these issues to a greater or lesser degree but it will continue to be an ongoing process in my life and I know that. It can take years for certain things to be ironed out and healing to happen. Being gentle in our own lives and in dealing with others is a wonderful way to start healing. Everyone makes mistakes and no one is perfect. When we start to see that in our own self-reflection, it makes a big difference as to how we treat others.

    The amount of changes that had taken place around me at times had been overwhelming. I had met other people that had their own spiritual gifts and talents. Obviously, everyone's spiritual path is different and I have to respect others journey as well. I have had clients come to me that felt lost and incapable of using their own gifts because of things had been said to them. I have experienced this myself. I thought that God had taken away the gifts that he had given to me. I had listened to others and to their words instead of my own heart. It was very confusing but I believed them, at least for a while, but I let them prey on my low self-esteem. When it comes from people that you love and respect it can be even more hurtful and destructive. I had to take a long hard look at myself for a while and then learn to trust my own heart, instincts and intuition again. It wasn't easy, but it was worth it. I learned that angelic help is for everyone, no matter what your belief or religion. Just be open to God's angels your spirit guides and always thank them when they help.

There are ways to know if you are being guided in a Divine way. One of the first ways to tell is that it is never in the form of anything negative. It will be loving, gentle, compassionate and for the highest good of all. When I am guided from the angels or from the spirit realm, it is a quiet voice and it is not my voice. It is important to be cautious when being guided. Being guided should always be positive, no matter what the situation. It is not harmful or spiteful to anyone in any way. It is given for good and if the words of guidance you receive are of blame or accusation about people around you or negative about yourself then it is not Divine guidance.

While doing this work, it is so important to be protected. You must ask for help from your own guardian angel and spirit guides of God's love. Always ask who it is that is guiding you, and that they must leave if what you are receiving is dark or negative. When I am aware of having a deceased person contacting me, I always ask to be protected. Then I say three times, "In the name of Our Lord Jesus, who are you and what do you want?" If they are there for the wrong reasons, at the sound of Jesus' name being said three times, they have to leave. I do this because the darkness is always trying to look for a way in, but I trust God and in my angels and spirit guides to keep the dark at bay.

I believe that while doing this work, tests and challenges can arrive. The evil in the world can work in very subtle ways to create doubt and fear. Friends that did not know this side of me are very surprised when I let them know what I do now in my life. I have received lots of different reactions as I have said before. Some good, some bad but I do not let it bother me as I did at the start. Self-acceptance is an important quality in order to have peace. Worrying about the opinions of others, loved ones or not, is only destructive. It is of much greater importance to me to be able to help people than to think of how I am viewed because of what I do.

It takes courage to stand in truth, and I have to say I am blessed with such wonderful friends and family, heavenly and earthly to help me do this. Making the decision to write this book was a difficult choice. It's not that I wanted people to know about me, it's to let people know how much help they have from heaven and from God's angels.

Signs from Heaven come to us all the time, like when you think about a loved one who has passed away. Most people don't realise that they are thinking of them because they are right there in that moment. Signs come in all forms; it can be a song, a smell, a photo falling, or a word you keep seeing or hearing over and over. These things are used to connect you to memories of your deceased loved ones.

I am very aware of how much people hold on to sadness, worry and sometimes guilt. I had said to some of my clients as an exercise, "See yourself sitting on a fence, watching life going by. You have two powerful angels on each side waiting to help you. You are holding on very tightly to the past, the negative events that surround you. I know you have asked for help over and over, and you think no one is listening, but you have a beautiful guardian angel who hears you and see's you. Look at it as if you have big, black bin liners full of all your fears, worries and huge doubts. Then see yourself letting go of that bag full of your terror and problems whatever they may be. Your angels and spirit friends cannot pry it from your hands. Remember that you have free will, you must want to let go." When you let go see a beautiful path light up in front of you, take your guardian angel's hand and walk forward not looking back. See all the things you would wish for your life on that path, whatever it is you need mentally, emotionally, psychically, spiritually or materialistically. See your dreams appear and thank God and His angels for their help in bringing these wonderful things into your life. Be thankful and grateful, bring faith, hope and love into the vision and it is complete and a wonderful way to start anew every single day.

    I see people hold and carry their problems in this way. I am not saying that this always works and helps instantly or every time, but it is a start to looking at life's problems from a different perspective. I ask them to try and let go and leave it all down and to see themselves getting off the fence to start walking a new path with their amazing angelic friends. On that new path see the things blooming that you want in your life should it be good health, a new house, more laughter, a new job and so on. Thinking of your worries and woes in this way, and that they can be left down no matter what problem it is, if it is addictions, vices of any kind you're battling or your health, etc., this is a good start for healing and happiness to begin. Sometimes it is hard for some to let go. Perhaps they have carried baggage for a long time and have started to think of it as normal. I have watched clients sitting in front of me, doing this small exercise and bringing great release. It can be emotional and they have said to me, "I feel different and lighter, sort of giddy!" This is really the angel's powerful healing coming to them and what happens while doing my spiritual work.

A Heavenly Gift

Pauline Johnson

CHAPTER 12

Instincts & Intuition

I had been living in my log cabin now for nearly a year. I was also starting to do psychic work for strangers, which would always make me nervous and at times filled me with doubt. I picked up a lot of intense feelings from the people around me. I began to empathise with their emotional state, whether they were sad, tired, irritated, I would begin to feel that way too. Because of this, it was not so easy being in a crowd of people. I did not realise at this time how important it was to protect myself from other's energies. My instincts and intuition where getting sharper, but doing my spiritual work left me very tired. I planned a trip back to Austria again in March for a break. I was just going with some friends and my brother Nigel, not the big group of friends I usually met up with. I was really looking forward to taking a break for a week.

We arrived on a Saturday evening to the beautiful Austrian village of Zell am See and got settled in. The next day, in the evening, I walked into a bar in the village and as I got inside I noticed that there were certain people whose faces changed. It was shocking and I had never experienced anything like it before. It was not everyone, just a few people, but their features changed, to what I can only describe as being like a werewolf. When I looked again, everything returned to normal. It was very disturbing and I was quite shaken by it. I had so many questions going on in my head after this happened. I learned later from the angels that what I had seen had more to do with a reflection of the person's soul. It is like they have forgotten or lost the love and compassion for themselves and others around them. It was not the last time I would see it either. I have seen it happen now about five times and it never fails to scare me. Recently I watched a show on TV called Grimm, I have to say it is similar to what I've seen, in how people change and how they look when they do. I know some of you will think I've embellished the story but, incredible as it may seem, these are all true experiences.

We carried on with our holiday, but it was not easy for me to forget seeing those faces. It made me much more aware of what people were like around me. We went skiing during the next day and it was a beautiful day. I had been going to Zell am See for years but I was seeing things I had never noticed before. In the mountains I could see beautiful female faces and figures in the contours of the rock. I even have the photos that show it. I know it is common to find shapes and faces in natural things, like the clouds and trees, but this was on such an enormous scale and in such detail. It was breathtaking and was a welcome sight from the ugliness of the night before.

The evening arrived and we went out again. I was in the bar waiting on a friend, who was in conversation with a guy we all knew well. I was sitting a bit away from them and suddenly another man came in and sat down at my table, right in front of me. I thought this was a bit weird there were lots of free seats available. I was getting up to leave and this man caught my hand. When I looked at him I was afraid, his eyes were totally black. I was again shocked, as I had never seen a person with eyes like that before. I did not want to look at him anymore and I immediately asked Archangel Michael to come to help me. It was instinctual to do that at this particular moment. I pulled my hand away just as my brother Nigel walked into the bar. The man looked at Nigel with such hate. I knew this person in front of me was completely shrouded in dark energy. I went to leave with Nigel and the man stood up, he must have been around six foot five. I had not really noticed his height when he arrived. He tried to stop me leaving and kept asking me to stay, but I just continued walking away from him with Nigel, I had no intention of staying around. I am very aware of how the dark and evil in the world will try to stop anything of good and light. It can come to us in many forms and sometimes can even be seen very clearly in people, as in this man. As we walked away, Nigel explained how he had got the feeling that he should go back to the bar. It came on suddenly and he felt that it was urgent though he didn't know why, but he knew he was being told to go check on us.

Archangel Michael works in wonderful protective ways and he needs more of the men of the world to be aware of him and to call for his help and guidance here on earth. I am sure he was guiding Nigel that night to come and look for us. When we have the protection of Heaven, we need not fear the dark. It was to be a year of learning to trust my own instincts and intuition and of knowing that I was looked after more than anything else. It had been an eye opener of a holiday in so many new spiritual ways in what I had seen in people and in nature.

When we arrived home from the holiday I was certainly glad to be home again. I needed to just have some peace and quiet for a while. I was still doing some photography and had sold some framed landscapes to the local shops. I love going out to walk to take landscape photos. I can spend hours outdoors doing this sort of photography. In Northern Ireland we have such incredible beauty to enjoy. Between photography and psychic work I was starting to create my own career. I did not charge at this time for psychic work and I was not making much money. It was a bit of a struggle to say the least, but I got by.

I could feel the connection to my angels and guides getting stronger every day. I was getting clearer messages and knowledge to help others, but then it suddenly changed. I started getting some negative feedback again at this time. It was from people I really cared about. I looked at them as very special with wonderful gifts. I was listening to voices of others telling me I was wrong and to stop what I was doing and for a time I truly believed this. I was totally confused. I held on to what they said more than trusting what I felt. Doubt set in and I stopped doing spiritual work and closed down. I felt very lost in a way. I still carried on with the photography and tried to put the spiritual side of things down. It was difficult, my self-esteem was at an all-time low, but I also had the strongest feeling that I had not lost anything. It was not long until I was brought back to my angels again. It was small things at first. I was still picking up on how people were feeling around me and I was still seeing orbs of light around people. These things let me know my angels and guides were still with me. I also started to hear my name being called. Soon I went and got myself new cards and started afresh. Immediately, in positive affirmation, I started to have a lot of contact from the spirit world. I could be anywhere; shopping, cooking or even driving. I would hear different voices and names and it became clearer as time went by. It worked out that having that break away from the spiritual side of my life was very enlightening and cleansing for me in lots of positive ways at that time. It all took off again in a beautiful way.

  I have explained how I feel the spirit of a deceased person trying to come through. I get a pain that can come to either side of my head. If it is to the left side they are young, ranging from children to people in their forties. If it is to the right, it's from people who are older. As they would connect to me, I would always hear their name and they would request prayers. It could be one prayer or even a decade or two of the rosary. Whatever they needed, I would stop what I was doing to help these spirits in need. I did not mind at all. In my mind's eye, I could see these spirits as they requested prayers. To me they seemed to be wearing grey robes, shimmering and pale. Once I would say the prayers for them though, they would change from grey to brilliant white robes, and they all looked so bright, joyful, happy, peaceful and young, then they would start fading, floating upwards away from me.

I wondered though, why they were asking me for prayers, and I soon had a reply. I was shown a long line of people in a queue, waiting for prayers to take them to Heaven. I was amazed at what one prayer could do for a spirit in this way. There were many queues of people waiting on prayers, all of different ages. I have always as a child said the prayer for the souls in purgatory. I do not know if it was purgatory that I was shown, but I do know that prayers are helping those people. The prayer I have said since childhood is a simple prayer, but I realise now how important it is and how much it is needed to help these souls. Any prayer said from the heart will help. The beauty and power of a prayer said in this way has a truly spectacular outcome.

The short prayer for the souls in Purgatory

*"Please God relieve the poor suffering
souls in Purgatory."*

Prayer of St Gertrude the Great

*Eternal Father, I offer thee
the most precious blood
of thy divine son, Jesus
in union with the masses
said throughout the world today
for all the Holy Souls in Purgatory,
for sinners everywhere,
for sinners in the universal Church
and those in my own home and family.*

When the Lord's angels are close, things feel totally different. It is more of a warm tingling feeling, like being wrapped in a cozy quilt, totally safe and happy. You need to work on your vibration to make you more aware of their guidance. Being positive, gentle, quiet and happy does help, as well as keeping your thoughts and emotions in balance. The angel's vibration is much higher than the vibration of the spirit realm, but both are blissfully wonderful in different ways.

I had been given lots of messages and now knew more about the spirit guides that were helping me. Archangel Raphael gave me most of the details of my guides and other angels and what they would be with me for. Archangel Michael has also given me very powerful messages of direction and help. Of course, I had Merlin that I described a little earlier, who was always loving and so powerful. I always felt totally protected when he was with me. Then I was given the names of John, Beth, and Bearl. I was introduced to John. He is American, so handsome and from the sixties. He is young and so relaxed. He has a wonderful, youthful energy and there is such love and gentleness from him. He helps me with all the younger deceased. John is always at hand when I have people that have lost children and teenagers. Beth and Bearl are both Native American and help me stay strong and positive. The last spirit guide I was introduced was Mat. Mat was introduced to me in a very unusual way but that is another story. Mat guides and helps me receive clear messages when dealing with the older deceased and for messages to help the people that come my way. He is again very loving, protective and powerful. Mat has an unusual appearance and is so tall and gentle. These are my main spirit guides. They are very loving, beautiful and my friends from God. My guardian angel Serena had other angels to introduce me to as well. Angel Matthew for direction and prayer in my life but also to help other people and their direction in life, Angel Carrie for strength, Angel Elixir for comfort, Angel Victoria and Angel Gabriel for music. Again, each angel would help with different aspects of helping and healing people that are sent my way. My job is just to get out of their way and let the healing come through. I have been very blessed and have amazing help to do what I do.

    This was the start of me knowing to trust in myself again, and that, when doing spiritual work it is so important to invite help, protection and guidance from Heaven. If you are a person with a poor self-image it can be so hard to gather yourself up and get going. For me, I just started to trust what I was feeling again. Trust your gut instincts, your own body will give you more insight if something is right or wrong. For example: if you are in a place that does not seem safe, you may get a warning in the form of a sinking feeling in your stomach, your temperature may feel a bit erratic, or you get feeling of goose bumps all over. Pay attention to what your senses are telling you and trust how you feel about them.

If a person close to you is belittling or negative to you, it reveals far more about them than you. Forgiveness can be hard in this kind of situation, especially if they are family or friends. Everyone sees things from their own point of view. I think the best thing to do is to forgive them, but also apologise for any wrong doing on your part, then send love and blessings in your thoughts and prayers and let it go. Being gentle with yourself is equally important to start to heal.

I was soon on track, but being positive and happy was something that needed constant work at this time. As my confidence was growing, I decided that I needed a place where I could do spiritual work for people. My living room was not really the ideal place, so I kept an eye out for ideas. Life was starting to move again for me. I had not been in a relationship for a long time and I missed it. Every now and then I went out with my brother Brendan. It was always fun and it got me out of the house for a bit. I was in more control of my eating disorder and I was back to my normal weight. I was so happy in my cabin and things were much more peaceful, however I was still battling with the settlements and the annulment. It was a a slow process, but at least things were moving in the right direction. Mum and I would go to Donegal to stay every so often. I had a little money coming to me each week and had sold some photos so, one week we headed off to Pollyanna's Cottage.

We arrived and got settled in and the next day we had decided to visit a shrine to Our Lady that we had heard about. I had no idea that there were so many shrines to Our Lady in Donegal. I came across three or four, but none was the one we were looking for. I drove around for quite a bit and then we called it a day and started to head back to the cottage. We were a little disappointed, but we had lovely weather and the scenery as always is beautiful. We arrived back and pulled up to the front of the cottage, as I got out of the car a medal fell onto the ground. I thought it was my mother's, so I said to her, "Mum there is your medal." Mum was still in the car, I turned to give it to her but there was another one on my car seat. I lifted the second medal and thought mum must have two of these. I said, "Here, you dropped these."

She looked confused, "They must be yours, they are not mine."

I took a closer look, but I knew they weren't mine. They were both miraculous medals.

The history of the miraculous medal is that a sister of charity called Catherine Laboure in 1830 received the vision of this medal from Our Lady. The medal has a prayer written on it: *Oh Mary, conceived without sin, pray for us who have recourse to thee.* When Catherine Laboure received the vision, Our Lady told her that anyone who wears this medal will receive great graces, especially if they wear it around their neck. Many miracles have come to those who have worn it. Health had been restored, dangers averted, bad habits overcome, and souls converted. As I was looking at the medals, the most beautiful voice came to me. It was a female voice and said, "You do not have to look for me, I am with you always." I knew then that we do not have to go to a certain place to find Our Lady or drive around for miles looking for particular places. It was a powerful confirmation for me. That the medals appeared out of nowhere was astonishing on its own, but to receive a message from Our Lady was more than I could ever have hoped for. It gave me the greatest feeling of peace and happiness and of heading in a good direction in my life.

It was also at this time being at Pollyanna's I got to see my deceased brother Noel. I was walking back towards my car from the beach one evening and I thought, *someone is sitting in my car!* I felt a sense of panic, but as I got closer I just knew it was Noel. He looked so much like my older brother Brendan it was uncanny. I could only stare as I walked to the car but the closer I got the more faded he became and then he was gone. I got a message when I reached for the car door handle, *he really likes your car,* that message made me smile, *Ah,* I thought, *another car freak in the family.*

CHAPTER 13
Grounding & Growing

It was 2005 and I was doing really well on a lot of levels. I was living in my cabin and still trying to get my photography business off the ground. It was challenging, but it was also something to keep me busy. I was also doing loads of jobs around the house. There was still painting to be done and the outside of the cabin needed a lot of work. There were bushy juniper trees surrounding the house and they had grown a bit out of control and stood about twenty feet tall. They really needed to be cut down and taken away if I was to have any room for a garden, so when my two amazing nephews arrived Darren and Emmett to start cutting I was happy to let them get to it. It was not an easy job and I was really grateful for their help but they are always there for me when I need them. My nephews had made great progress cutting back the trees, I had not realised how much garden there was.

I was still doing the usual rounds of annulment and court meetings. It was so normal to me now I was less bothered by them with each appointment. I would hear from my husband every so often. It was sad because the people that I had thought of as friends were no longer there. These are people that I had spent weekends and holidays with. Anytime they visited my home when I had been married, they were treated so well. I never uttered a wrong word to them but when a breakup happens it all changes in a dramatic way. Although a divorce was between just the two people that were married, it was like dropping a pebble into a pond. The ripples went out so much further and, unfortunately, it is very common in this kind of situation for people to take sides and judge. For me, I did not really want to see other people there was always too many questions and too many people being more nosey than truly concerned. I was trying to get over depression, eating problems, worry and fear. I would hear what was being said from time to time and the things I was hearing back were so far from the truth it was ridiculous, but sometimes people would rather believe lies over the truth.

Doing spiritual work for people gives me a lot of insight into how people truly feel when they have to make difficult choices. I have had many people who have been confused or troubled as a result of readings or 'alternative therapies' they have had done for them. Just like the next story.

I had a beautiful girl called Imelda come to me that was in some distress. Imelda was a very spiritual person with great belief in God and His angels. She had been going to a person that she called a Reiki healer. Now, I have to say that I have never been to a Reiki session so I do not know anything about how it is done. Imelda had been told by her Reiki practitioner that she needed to go for an appointment every week. By the time she came to see me it had been going on for about a year and a half and she told me that her situation was going from bad to worse. Imelda explained that, at the start she had felt good but then that feeling had stopped and other parts of Imelda's life and health had began taking a turn for the worse. I was not long into my visit with Imelda when my guardian angel Serena brought her granny through. She had come to let Imelda know that she is never alone and tell her to have strength. Imelda told me her granny had been a very strong woman and that she wanted to be more like her. I know she is more like her granny than she knows and will realise it increasingly as she heals. I was guided to let Imelda know that she should not go back to this person that was telling her that she needed weekly treatments. The Reiki "healer" who was manipulating her energy in the wrong way had created her distressed state. My angels and guides told me to recommend professional counselling after this, which I happily did.

A wonderful healing usually happens while people are with me, and it comes from God's angels. It is like the angels lift a heavy veil or weight from people, and they begin to feel lighter and have a sense of hope. Often people come to me looking for a cure for the problems in their lives. The angels and guides give perspective on a situation, but ultimately it is up to the person to make the choice to change. In Imelda's case, she had sought help from a questionable source and only ended up compounding her problems. Be careful who you put your trust in to help you if you are in a vulnerable state or who you give permission to manipulate your energy. I was aware of how the angels had guided her to me to get through to her, but it was ultimately her decision to start to heal and to trust the strength she has within to help herself. I have heard from Imelda since then and she is doing better. The path of healing and change is not an easy one, but I continue to keep her in my prayers.

I was doing psychic work for so many more people now and slowly the word was getting out. It was still very low key, but I was grounded in knowing what I needed to do. Building my life slowly again in a solid way made a lot of sense. It seemed at a snail's pace sometimes which was frustrating. I knew I still needed the right place and to manifest that I had to have clarity and a positive attitude. Divine timing is important and I knew this was the time to have trust and belief. I believe that if we look too far ahead to the future, we will miss the blessings in the present and the beauty and magic of each day. This was how it was for me and I assure you, I was not always happy to wait, but I could be excited about what would happen next.

I was spending a lot more time with my mum. We would go out for the occasional drive or shopping trip, which every one knows can sometimes be the best therapy. One day we had gone out on one of our shopping trips to Belfast. It was a normal day out just browsing the shops and having a coffee. Belfast can be very busy and it was no different on this particular day. We had just finished having lunch and decided to walk back to the car to head home. My mother was walking on my left and slightly in front of me when something made me turn and look at her and as I turned back, everything in front of me went into slow motion.

A group of girls were coming in the opposite direction. I put my arm out and pulled my mum back just in time to miss the point of an umbrella hitting her in the face. Two of the girls that were coming towards us had started fighting. My mother is in her eighties and would not have been able to move out of the way. It was an awful spectacle to see. One was swinging her umbrella at the other and they were pulling out each other's hair by the handfuls. It had all started so quickly, my mother was more shocked than I was. When the fighting had reduced to a screaming match, Mum and I quickly walked past.

Mum said, "How did you know to pull me back?"

I just replied, "Thank God I did!"

I always know that when things slow down around me like that, that it's time to pay attention and be open to instruction from my angels and guides. I was so happy that day that my mother did not lose an eye or have a bad facial cut to deal with. It was so disturbing to watch two females fighting. They had so much aggression and hate for each other. It was awful to watch this happen, but it is also how the darkness uses people in the world to harm other innocent people around them. Females are usually known for being gentle, compassionate, and caring. Those qualities are very much needed from the females in our world these days to balance the aggression that is so prevalent. It just makes seeing that kind of behaviour all the more sad.

Doing the work I do helps me to be more aware of what is going on around me in a more grounded way. I am so grateful to the Lord for giving us all a guardian angel to always be there, protecting and guiding us. It's important to just pause every day and acknowledge their help and their presence and to invite them into our every day lives. A common question I get is, "What do you say to your guardian angel?" I have used the same prayer that I was taught as a child the words are simple:

Guardian Angel Prayer

Oh Angel of God my Guardian dear,
To whom Gods love commits me here
Ever this day and night,
Be at my side, to light and guard,
To rule and guide, Amen.

Pauline Johnson

CHAPTER 14
Traveling & Trusting

I had traveled quite a bit in my life up until now. I have always enjoyed going to different countries and seeing new things. I have never had a bad trip or holiday. Maybe it's because I don't expect too much when stepping into an unknown country. I was thinking of going on a trip, but had not really decided where or when. I was living very quietly, maybe that is why I was getting an itch to go and travel a bit. I was also thinking I wanted some romance in my life again. I had been on my own for a while now and I wanted to have fun and feel loved. It was something that was very much lacking in my life. We all need to balance things in our lives it cannot be all worry, all work or all play. Earlier that year I was out one night with my brother and I told him very matter-of-factly, "I am going to meet an American rock singer, and he is going to be really tall and handsome, just wait and see." He just laughed and slagged me as usual. Little did I know at the time that I was making a prediction.

My travels thus far had mostly centred around Europe and I had been to so many beautiful places there. I had visited most of the European countries and I had friends in Sweden, Austria and Germany, but I decided I was going in the opposite direction this time. I had been to America once before. While I was married we took a trip to California. America is such a vast place, so this trip I decided to go to Seattle and then on to little town called Coeur d'Alene, in Idaho. You may wonder why I choose this particular destination. Well, it all took off one day while I was online as usual, when up on the computer screen popped the words 'online dating'. I am not one to be easily steered in a direction that seems silly or foolish, though I have my moments. I looked at this and thought,

A Heavenly Gift

So this is the new way to find love in this world today. My opinion, like a lot of other people at this time, was that it was ridiculous to try and find love looking at a computer.

I must have walked past the screen at least twenty times until finally, I sat down and started to read about it. It was a totally alien concept to me, but the more I read, the more feasible it seemed so I logged on and filled in my details. I took it casually. To me it was a bit of fun and I was sure that nothing would come of it. I didn't add a picture of myself or give much away because I was also a bit apprehensive of what might come back. This way of meeting people was all so new and uncertain. I closed the computer for the evening and got on with the rest of the things I had neglected to do. Starting up the computer in the morning it was the last thing in my mind but when I went to my email I had two hundred messages waiting for me from the dating site! I was quite shocked these people did not even know what I looked like! Some of the messages were very funny. There were no bad messages, just people looking for love in their lives. I scanned over the photos of the men that had emailed me I had no idea that so many people were online doing this. It was a total surprise. I could send anyone a message or see all of their details. I had ticked the box on the website that the candidates could be from anywhere in the world, so that is where I got messages from - everywhere in the world!

The bulk of messages came from males in America, which was also quite surprising. I was looking through all of the photos that came along with their messages, but there was only one photo that caught my eye. He was attractive and very articulate in the way he wrote about himself. It made very interesting reading so, my finger poised above the mouse, I thought about clicking the hello button. Well, I wrestled with that decision for about two hours! I thought, *Don't be daft he could be a complete psycho!* All the things I was reading about him could be totally false and besides, he is so far away. It was then that I thought about what I was doing and began to laugh at my own fears. All of this because of a little button on my computer, so I pushed the hello button and put it out of my mind.

The next morning I got the computer going and was again not really expecting much. Of course I had received a reply, but it was not the answer I expected. It read, "You don't have a photo. I had mentioned in my details I do not want anyone messaging me that does not put their photograph up." And to top it all he ended his reply with "And you are older than me. I clearly posted 'my age or younger.'"

Well I thought, *How rude is this guy!* But then I thought, *Maybe I do need to put a photo up. It's a bit absurd to expect people to message me when there is no face to put to the words.*

So I uploaded a photo, still feeling a bit miffed at the response I had received, after all, all I did was say hello. I closed the computer for the day and got on with other things, still thinking to myself, *Pauline are you are being daft*, but I had the distinct feeling that I should keep going and trust my instincts. Again I waited until the next day to check if anything new had happened. I have to say I was more apprehensive than the day before. I had over four hundred messages waiting for me, including one from the guy I thought was so rude. He had written, "You're beautiful! Is this really you?" I thought, *Oh, so he thinks I am beautiful now*. Well it was nice that he thought that, I didn't feel beautiful in any way at this time, but I did make him wait on the reply for a while that day. I had so many messages I could not believe it, so I only answered the ones I wanted to. It was still strange for me to connect with men in this way. Still, I hadn't dated in years, so it was kind of fun doing it from the comfort of my own home. The nice thing about it was that the men that had contacted me were polite and friendly instead of drunk and spitting out bad one-liners. I only replied to three messages that first evening, including the first guy. He was now being completely different since he had received my photo. In truth, he was as wary as I was about the whole online dating thing. I think everyone is. It's the unknown and you have to trust what is written more than anything else. Without going into long explanations of what happened while being on this dating site, the first guy I had said the dreaded hello to ended up staying in touch. He gave me his phone number and email address and we started to really get to know each other. He was graphic designer and a musician. We would chat online for hours and not notice the time passing. It was so incredible to have met in this way and have it seem so easy to connect over such a long distance. Of course the main obstacle was the distance between us, we were six thousand miles apart. I was looking at this to see if there is a way forward instead of worrying about the details of why it couldn't work. Finally, we decided we wanted to meet up to see what would happen. He was excited about meeting me and I felt exactly the same. It is a totally different thing to chat on a phone line than to stand in front of someone and be in their presence. I already knew that I wanted to take a holiday to the states. I had looked up the places I was going to visit and it was so fascinating. My planned route would take me to Chicago, Seattle, Spokane and then Coeur d'Alene. It would be six thousand miles and around twenty-three hours of travelling if it all went to plan.

It was a much bigger trip than I had ever taken before, and I was going alone. I knew a few people in America and had relations in Seattle, but I was not planning on visiting with them. I wanted to see new places and experience new people. I just felt that this new direction I was being taken in was the right one. I had booked my holiday for August. Some of my family thought I was a bit mad going all the way to a new place on my own. I wasn't worried about it though I have travelled alone on trips abroad quite a few times and always had a wonderful time. I also trust that I am being guided and looked after. My guardian angel and guides are always with me no matter where I go.

Travel has always been a big part of my life. I had travelled at length in Europe and most of the islands around Europe, but no matter how much I travel, the most wonderful place for me is still Ireland. It has such mystery and wild beauty. There is nowhere that I have been that is more beautiful to me. The people and food here in Northern Ireland are wonderful. It's one of the reasons I enjoy taking photos and walking in nature at home, no matter what the weather is like. Still, I was looking forward to seeing what the North West of America had to offer. It did not take long for the day of my journey to arrive. I had to fly from Dublin to London. It just so happened the weekend I had chosen to fly out was the same weekend that all the bomb scares had taken place in London over the week. *Oh great,* I thought, *there would be total chaos in all the airports and this long trip is going to take even longer.*

When I arrived into Dublin airport, security was in full force. As someone from Northern Ireland security always takes a bit longer, but this time customs and passport control took twice as long. I was dreading Heathrow, it is always so busy and packed no matter when you go. When I arrived, it was much worse than I could have imagined. There was a hill of luggage in middle of the terminal floor about forty feet high and a hundred feet wide, I had never seen anything like it. It was all the luggage from previous flights that had been cancelled, sitting there waiting to be sorted. People where sleeping everywhere. I thought, *Oh God, am I going to have cancelled flights too!* I had loads of interconnecting flights to catch at certain times along my route and all of those were going to have to be rebooked. I could be travelling for days! Fearing the worst I went to my check in desk only to find a massive queue. I thought, *This is going to take forever*, but then one of the airline staff came over to me and asked me where I was going. I was surprised that of all the people in the queue, she had come to me. I explained where my final destination was and that I had connecting flights to get. Well, to my astonishment, she pulled me to the front of the queue and checked my baggage straight through to Spokane. I was stunned and so grateful. She told me I would not see my bags or need to worry about them as they would go through all my destinations with me. I was whisked through passport control quickly it wasn't until I was standing in my departure area that I fully realised I was on my way. There had been thousands of people sitting, waiting, sleeping in the check in areas just trying to get where they were going. Miraculously, I had no problems with any of that. Before I knew it, I was boarding the flight to Chicago. I don't know if it was Angels, guides or the miraculous help of Our Lady, but I know that God helped me that day, as he does everyday, just sometimes not in such a visible way.

I arrived into Chicago airport after eight hours of a flight. You don't realise how big the Atlantic Ocean is until you fly over it! I was so excited to be doing this trip that I was not even tired. I had now to get a connecting flight from Chicago to Seattle. Chicago's O'Hare airport is massive, but again, I got through it quite quickly. The layover gave me a bit of time to just relax and get something to eat. Soon I was on my way across the expanse of America. I arrived into Seattle and had to go through so many terminals, it took quite a while. Somehow I ended up going through security on the wrong side. I was a bit lost and asked directions from a security man. When I got to the passport control I realised I was on the other side of it all. When I went to the security people for them to check my passport, they could not believe I had got through without going through them. I thought it was quite funny, but they thanked me for coming to them. There was a bit of a commotion when I explained how I had arrived to their passport control area. It seems there were some doors left unsecured. They scrambled security personnel to fix the problem and thanked me again. Seattle's SeaTac airport is a very busy place and eventually I was on my way to Spokane, it was only a one-hour flight from Seattle. I arrived into Spokane airport and as I walked down the ramp I saw Monte for the first time. The date was the 20th of August, how ironic.

CHAPTER 15
Loving & Living

I had no clue at this time that my trip to America would last for three months. I had gone to have a holiday and to see a new place, but it ended up so much more. When I woke the next day to see the town I was in awe, it was so beautiful. I had arrived in darkness so I only saw lots of lights and nothing else. There where no skyscrapers here, even though I had expected to see a lot of them. Coeur d'Alene is in the northern panhandle of Idaho, close to the Canadian border. Idaho has the Rocky Mountains running through it, and borders Montana, Wyoming, Oregon, Washington, Utah, Nevada and British Columbia in Canada. I had no idea it was going to be so beautiful. I had looked at it online of course, but to be standing in a place is totally different.

The city of Coeur d'Alene is surrounded by forested mountains and a massive freshwater lake spanning over twenty-five miles. In places it is almost two-thousand feet deep. The lake was spectacular; with all the boats and a marina to walk around and to top it all, I had at last met Monte. The incredible thing was, the words I had used to tell my brother nearly a year before meeting him about what my new boyfriend would be like, described Monte completely. Although he was a graphic designer, it turned out he was also a rock singer in a band called Kite, American, six foot three, and so handsome I was really in a bit of shock.

We ended up spending most of my holiday time doing things together and being so relaxed in each other's company. I am not saying that online dating is for everyone but it turned out fine for me! It is important to be careful when going into any new situation and to make sure you are in a public place when meeting someone new. When traveling like I was, alone, you must also have other things sorted out like where you are staying and that your loved ones at home know where they can contact you. We got on so well from the first time we met it was great. Even though all these signs were a bit incredible to take in, I was still very cautious. It takes some time to get to know someone, but I soon realised that he thought exactly the same way. It made it all a lot easier to take time and do things together without expecting a relationship. I had such a wonderful time that as it got close to the time I was supposed to leave, Monte asked me if could I stay longer. I didn't need much encouragement and ended up staying for three months.

This was to be the beginning of love in my life and the start of living my life in a new way. We both had come through some difficult times in life with regard to relationships. It is sometimes hard to leave down old baggage we carry from past relationships. At some stage, we all end up with a zero tolerance for certain behaviour. I didn't realise until I met Monte how many things I needed to let go of. Old hurts, fears, worries and pain seem to come to the surface in the face of a new relationship. A lot of it comes from a fear of the emotions that make us close our heart down. To love again and put yourself out there, to be vulnerable and open, in a position of having all those feelings flood back, is never easy. It takes time and courage to want love back into your life, but at the same time, it makes us feel more alive and present when we do. It's important to recognise that courage comes in many forms, like in the case of Jim who made an appointment to came to see me for a reading and discovered that there was more in his way than he initially thought.

No one wants to go through life alone and Jim was no exception, he wanted to know about love coming into his life. He was in his fifties, had a good job and his own house and he just wanted someone to share it all with. He had been in a relationship for a few years but even though it had ended, his ex-girlfriend would still expected him to be available when she needed him to help her. This included everything from her bills to her whole life in general. Jim was very good-natured and did his best to help her out, but he had just spent many years caring for his parents before they passed away and he wasn't interested in having to do the same for his ex. When he came to me, it was obvious when the guides and angels came through that he needed to leave the past behind before he could move into the future. There had been family issues as well with land and property that, unfortunately didn't end well. He was hurt deeply by the people that he had loved the most. The incident damaged Jim's ability to trust and his heart had closed down, now it had to be healed and opened again. The angels and guides brought the one person through for Jim that could help the most, his father. Jim had been a little skeptical when he arrived to me that day and the angels knew he would need some solid validation, so when I was told to ask him if he had been working on a tractor that week he looked at me totally surprised. I told him it was a red tractor and he was fixing something on the back part of the axle. I was also told to say that his deceased father still walked around the yard and that he liked the way he had tidied the shed. His father really liked that Jim had kept his walking stick in the same place in the corner of his house. I was given a description of all of these details so Jim would know I wasn't having one over on him. His father's walking stick was unique in that it was a two-toned stick and I went on to describe it to him. Jim couldn't believe it, all of the things had been done that week with the shed and the tractor were correct, and his father's walking stick was where it always had been and was exactly as described. Jim enjoyed his visit to me so much he comes back to me now about every nine months or so.

The second time Jim came to me the angels asked me to do a very special healing for him. I had to invite Archangel Raphael and Archangel Uriel in to help heal his heart and body. It only took a few minutes to do but it helped Jim be more grounded and finally feel like he wasn't missing a part of himself. The healing was the start of the process to open and heal his heart to the love he wanted so badly to come into his life. Jim was very willing to have the healing done and he said he would let me know if the lady of his dreams comes along before I see him again. Jim knows he has certain changes to make to help him move forward, certain things he has to leave behind in a permanent way for the wonderful and the new to arrive. If we are wasting our energy and love on a person, place or thing in the past or present that is only using us for their own ends, then we need to ask ourselves if what we are doing is creating good or bad in our lives. Your angels and guides can help you to summon the courage to make changes in your life that you never thought possible. It's like the old saying goes: A miracle is what seems impossible but happens anyway. If you feel stuck then make a list of the good and bad things about the situation, it can be very enlightening when you see which list is longer. It is what Serena and Archangel Raphael told me to do to help me see clearly in lots of situations.

Being in America was wonderful. I found it so relaxing and it was great to have the time to explore and experience new things. I had been to America before, but this was so different. North Idaho has so much character. It has cool, quirky shops, galleries, loads of cafés and great restaurants and the people are really easy going. Each morning I went out and walked for miles. The weather was beautiful and the scenery breathtaking. It was such a breath of fresh air to feel this free I had not felt like that for years. Of course having Monte as my tour guide when he was off work was really great for both of us. We would go out on his lunch hour and go walking at the lake - the time would fly by.

Because I had not known Monte very long, I had not really told him much about my physic work or the experiences I had. He knew I did a bit of photography and thought that was all I did. I had no idea what his reaction would be, but he did need to understand more about me. Well, there can only be one of two reactions, normally it is, 'I don't believe in that.' or 'Really?' I don't mind what reaction I get, as long as I tell the truth. It has nothing to do with me how others react or what they may say or think. When I started to explain to him about what I do and what

I can experience at different times he was not surprised at all. He found it all fascinating, but it is one thing telling someone and another thing entirely when you show them, that can be a challenge as I found out.

One Saturday morning while doing laundry, I was in my room folding clothes, as everyone does. I had been in America now for about five weeks and not had any unusual experiences since getting so easily through all the airports. I also did have the usual spirits asking for prayers, so I did that as normal. This one particular morning though, I sensed a different kind of spirit was present around me. I could not see them as a full, manifested apparition, but I could see them visually in my mind. This was a female and she was trying so hard to let me know her name. I thought I could hear, Mary or Marie. It was so faint, but I got very still and asked her if she have a message or wanted prayers. She did not ask me for prayers, but did have a message for me to give to Monte. I thought, *I don't know how he's going to take this, but here goes.* I think there was a part of me that knew exactly how he would take this piece of information.

When I told Monte there was a female present and had a message for him, he was very skeptical to say the least. Part of the message was to be true, meaning be true to the person that he is, but the last part of the message was more personal between this spirit and Monte because the spirit was Monte's mother. Monte's mom had died in her late forties of bone cancer. I did not even know Monte's mother's name at this time, but it was Marie. The other part of the message was something only him and his mother knew of and it had happened while he was with her before she died. He was a bit upset that I had received a message so soon after meeting him. He had waited for years to have a sign of anything from her. He was quite taken back that I was standing there, all the way from Northern Ireland, telling him about things that there was no way I could know. I had to reiterate to him that it had nothing to do with me, that I was just the messenger. Heaven allows me to be able to hear and help convey what comes through.

I did say to him, "Believe what you have received or not, the message is not for me." Sometimes people say,

'That's cool that you do that', or, 'How unusual' but these gifts can cause strong reactions when it happens in every day life and the message or sign is personal. Monte understood and overcame his initial defensiveness, but it was not to be the last time that he would find himself a little surprised about my gifts.

I had come on this journey expecting to see yellow cabs and a lot of built-up areas but I was totally wrong. The houses were all so quaint, built of wood and planned out like bungalows in Ireland, but much prettier, with white picket fencing, and porches at the front. I was surprised to see all the pavement slabs broken because of the big trees that lined the streets. Their roots pushed up and broke them apart so when you walked, especially at night, you could stumble like a person that had a few drinks too many. There was so much to do and explore. In Idaho, they have millions of acres of ancient forest wilderness. It's nothing like the forest parks we have in Northern Ireland. They have grizzly bears, brown bears, moose, mountain lion, elk, and wolf, roaming free through the mountains. We rode Monte's motorcycle to see wolves and buffalo.

These were things I had only seen on a television screen and I was enthralled with all of it. Monte has a wide range of hobbies and professions; sword fighting, camping, shooting and music, to name just a few. We went to different events to do with each of these activities and they were all really distinct and interesting. A lot of the people he knew had heard of this woman from Ireland that he was seeing and we were invited to all kinds of parties and events. It was a bit of a whirlwind at times.

 A friend of Monte's invited us to dinner one evening and I was really looking forward to it. We arrived at their home and went out to the back yard to meet everyone. The weather is so nice there that they spend a lot of time eating and entertaining outdoors. I ended up sitting beside a girl that I had never met before, but when I turned to say hello, all I could see floating around her head and shoulders were images of witches. I know this sounds totally strange, but you should have been looking at it from where I sat. I could not believe my eyes for a few seconds. It was funny, but also surreal, I was seeing witches hats, black cats, faces and brooms. I looked away for a short time and when she spoke to me again and when I looked back, there they were. I just had to ask her, "Do you like witches and stuff like that?" She went silent, and stared at me for a minute. Then she asked me if anyone had mentioned that to me. I said, "No, I just wondered." It took about two seconds for her to leave her seat maybe it was a little quicker than that. Like the old saying, 'Jumping out of the way like a scalded cat', well it was more like that really. She then sat on the opposite side of the table looking at me and that was the end of our conversation for that night.

After I said this to her all the things I had seen were gone from around her. I think it was one of the funnier things I have watched when things open up around people. But I did learn later that she was very much into all aspects of witches and the history. I do not know a lot about witches, but when I did met her after that it was much more normal, or maybe her guard was up a little more around me. It was after that night that I would get a strong sense of that kind of similar energy around different females while being out and about in parts of Coeur d'Alene. The energy was quite strong and it seemed to me that I only felt it amongst females. It didn't bother me at all but it was interesting to say the least, and I only saw that vision once in all the time I was there.

Being with Monte was so new and exciting. I had not been in a relationship for a while and we where both treading carefully and slowly. I was looking forward to having him come over to Northern Ireland and see what he thought. In the middle of Coeur d'Alene, on the main street there was a shop called All Things Irish full of Irish souvenirs and clothing. I was really surprised to see an Irish shop and the lady that owned it was really wonderful. She had items from all over Ireland, so I would go into the shop with Monte and explain where certain things were made and how far away it was from where I lived in Co Tyrone. It was great to see a bit of Ireland in the middle of a town in Idaho. I was getting ready to come back home and was happy to be going back to Ireland. The three months had flown by, but I did not realise how much I would miss Monte not being around me every day. Good thing was he coming to Northern Ireland six weeks later.

A Heavenly Gift

Pauline Johnson

CHAPTER 16
Walls & Wonders

Flying over Ireland is always a wonder for me. It is such a green landscape, truly beautiful and majestic. I seem to forget how green it is compared to other countries, but it always feels like home no matter how long my time away is. I was sad leaving Monte in America and it had been a long trip back. It takes around twenty-two hours though it has more to do with waiting in airports than actual time in the air. I was glad when I finally touched down in Dublin. My brother Garry was there to meet me. It was great to see him and finally be heading home. Garry was chatting away and I fell asleep, I woke in the car outside my mothers, I had slept for nearly two hours. I had never experienced jet lag on that scale before. I had it when I arrived in America, then got it again on my return home. It can be the most unusual feeling. One minute you're full of energy and the next you need to sleep for hours. Idaho is eight hours behind us in time, so my internal time clock was all over the place. It takes about three weeks to start to feel grounded and normal again. I said my hellos to mum and then headed down to my cabin. I was so tired I slept until the next day. Waking up it took a bit of time to realise I was home.

I woke up to big changes to my outside garden. My nephews had not only trimmed back the trees they had removed them entirely! I realised for the first time how much garden I was going to have. At least they had left the two cherry blossom trees. It was all so wide and open I thought of putting a fence up, but I also knew how strong the winds could be so I decided that when I got the time to put something up, it should be a wall instead. It was so blissful to be back home, I was just in time to get things sorted for Christmas and Monte's visit. He was not going to be arriving until the week before Christmas. My head, of course was still full of the trip I had, but Monte was in my mind more than anything else. It had been such a whirlwind between us and it was still going. It made me happy to think about all of it.

I had a load of letters to go through and lots of things to sort from being gone for so long. Soon I was back to my usual round of meetings and details to sort out, but I felt happier than I had for a long time. My eating habits had greatly improved, but I am always aware that this kind of problem is one you carry every day in life. It has a lot to do with low self-esteem as I talked about earlier, or feeling you have no control. I will probably always worry about my weight. I know I'm not alone in that internal struggle thousands of people go through it just like me. It is when it becomes obsessive that it needs to be gently and lovingly healed. With a condition like this, similar to so many other types of illness, it is a good thing to remember you cannot run or hide from yourself. It requires you to have patience, understanding, love and time to accept, to repair the mind and body. Above all give yourself the present of self-acceptance give yourself more hugs, more gentleness and happiness instead of guilt and worry. Just like the story of Ruth that came for a reading.

There was a lady that came to me that had lost a child, and suffered a miscarriage before that. Ruth would shut her eyes in anguish while she was explaining her loss to me and my heart ached for her. When she had first arrived for the session I immediately picked up that she had lost a part of herself, I did not know that she had suffered loss twice over in such a short time. Her baby had been born but died four months later. It was a cot death and no reason was found to explain why it had happened as in most cases. Even though my heart went out to her as I listened, I had to be aware to keep my emotions balanced in order to help in a healing way. She was a wonderful mother to her two other children but she knew she was putting on a show each day. Ruth said that since the loss of her baby, she would get through each day like a robot. It was affecting her relationship with her husband and with her children. Everyone in her home was walking on eggshells, not talking about what had happened as a family. During her visit, Serena my guardian angel, Mat and John my spirit guides came through and they brought Ruth's grandmother with them. I could see her granny carrying an incredible light in her arms, cradling it lovingly and I knew right away that this was the angels bringing Ruth's baby to let her know he was in a wonderful place, with loving family members surrounding him. It was really a beautiful sight. The baby was so bright I could not see him through the light that shone with all the colours of the rainbow. When I explained to Ruth who was there and what I was being shown she just let her tears flow.

    Tears are such a part of what I do, they're not a show of weakness. To me they help clear and release built up sadness, worry, guilt and other destructive energies. For Ruth it was a very necessary healing to help her be more present in her own life and for her family. When we came to the end of Ruth's visit she told me she felt a lightness she had not felt for months. She also said that the ache around her heart had somehow eased a little and that she experienced a feeling that many other people have after coming to me. They feel lighter and more hopeful. The angels give them a tingling, warm energy that wraps around them. It is also from their loved ones essentially giving them what I can only describe as a spiritual hug. The angels can only heal as much as people allow them to. Releasing a lot of anguish takes time and patience. Ruth's family had been so supportive to her and she thought she was not able to give anything back it was from this that feelings of guilt crept in. Her angels and guides reminded her to be much more gentle with herself and to expect the array of emotions she was experiencing after such a traumatic event. Afterwards, Ruth asked me to ask the angels and guides why this had happened, why she had lost her child. I am not always able to receive an answer from questions like these but this day I did. In the case of Ruth's child I tried my best to put the explanation into words. The situation was arranged before the soul came to the family. The length of a person's life is sometimes predestined. God's plan for each person is different and we have no control over that, we just have to trust that his reasons are from an expression of goodness and love we cannot possibly comprehend. When Ruth came back to me a year later for another visit, she was much happier. She said that coming for the first time had done her so much good, it made her realise that she was needed and very loved. The family had come together more to get over the loss and though it had been hard they where getting through it in a slow but healing way. Everyone in the family was now much happier, especially because Ruth's energy was focused back on life and her family. The beautiful end to this story was the birth of Ruth's new baby boy two months before our second meeting.

The others things in my life were still on hold, but I had waited this long for them to move forward so a bit longer did not make much difference. At least they were moving towards completion and that was great. Sitting in my homely cabin, looking forward to Christmas and sorting out the details was exciting. It would be a very different Christmas for me because I had usually never spent a whole Christmas day with my husband. It was always me spending the day in my mother's and him spending the day in his mother's. The same would happen on New Years day as well. That went on for twenty-five years, but now I get to spend the whole day with Monte and the rest of the holiday as well. It would be his first taste of Ireland. In America, they have Thanksgiving in November, it is similar to how we celebrate Christmas day, but coming to Ireland is a trip a lot of Americans would love to make, so I was sure he was excited about coming here. When I had first spoken to the Monte's friends, their questions would eventually get around to what was it like to live in Northern Ireland. I know this is quite normal because of the world media coverage about the troubles we have experienced here. It is hard for people to understand what it is like living in a troubled country and some of the perceptions were very interesting. Some thought we were still traveling by donkey and cart. Now, that did make me laugh! I think that they must have watched the movie The

Quiet Man, too often. It can take a bit of explaining about how, through all the good and bad times, the people have stayed welcoming, positive and strong. I do recommend that, if you haven't visited Northern Ireland yet, to come and see how beautiful and historical it actually is. Monte was a bit apprehensive about it being a safe place to visit, but I assured him it had changed greatly from the times of the troubles.

I really got into the preparations and had the house all decorated with festive cheer and stocked to the nines, it was quite a bit of work, but it was Christmas, it's always worth it. I went to the airport and picked him up on the twenty second of December. He was as excited as I was. It had only been six weeks since I had seen him but it seemed longer. I knew he would be tired, so we went straight home. Having someone from another country being amazed at what we take for granted everyday does awaken appreciation of what we have around us. He said he had heard Ireland was very green, but he didn't expect it to be so literally true. It really does have forty shades of green. Everything was so new to him, the traffic of course being on the opposite side of the road took a bit of getting used to. The narrowness of some of the roads took him by surprise compared to the vast roads in America. I think it was a fascinating mix of old and new for him. Old in the way that Ireland is a much older country than where he came from and new in that it was much more modern than he had realised.

We got back home and chilled out for the first evening. We spent the day sorting out Christmas stuff that needed to be done. Everything being new and unfamiliar to Monte made it more fun; from the food, to the television channels, even the words we both use for different things and the way we pronounce them. It was quite amusing at times. The main thing was how much we enjoyed each other's company. I wanted Monte to have a restful first day. We were both so excited to be together again, it was hard to relax which, in itself was wonderful. Of course being in a new country makes you want to go out and explore as much as possible, but Monte was here in Northern Ireland for three weeks so he had plenty of time for that. My family all arrived and we met up in my mum's house. Monte got to meet them all at the one time. It is probably a little overwhelming to be surrounded by all my family at once, but they made him feel very relaxed. We went to Belfast to do some shopping later that week. It felt so great to be walking about Belfast, showing him the different places with all the buzz that is going on in the city at Christmas. Christmas Eve was really special, but then it always is. We had prepared a bit of food for that evening and then we had gone to mass. It was great to come home to spend time just sitting down after running around getting things sorted out over the previous three days. Mum was there with us and it made it really nice. It was a quiet lazy evening, but that is just what we all needed.

  Christmas day arrived and we had a great day opening presents, doing all the cooking, eating too much and all the things you do on Christmas. We ended the day with an unexpected crowd of my nephew's friends. It was a very late start the following morning. We decided to go to Donegal for a few days so he could see a different part of Ireland. I had told him so much about Pollyanna's Cottage that he couldn't wait to get there.

Now, I want to tell you why it's called Pollyanna's Cottage, and fill you in on the rest of the story. When I was born, my father named me Pauline Ann, and he would at different times when I was a child, call me Pollyanna. That part you already know. The other part is that my aunt telephoned my mother the same day I was born. Nothing strange about that, but she did not know what my father was going to name me. She suggested to my mum she should call me Polly Anna based on a new film she had just seen. So it seems that, one way or the other, I was going to be called Pauline Ann or Polly Anna.

Pollyanna's cottage is in a tranquil area of spectacular beauty overlooking Gweebara Bay. I also rent the cottage out in the summer months to holiday makers, once when I was on my way home from the cottage, I was driving through a village called Ardara. It's beautiful and quaint and not far from the cottage. I had driven past my turn off to Donegal Town without even realising it. I was a bit worried but finally I came to my senses and knew I had to turn around and get back on the correct route. I had only driven outside Ardara about two miles when I realised there was the spirit of a young girl in my car with me. I was told she needed not only prayers, but also encouragement to walk to the angels and into the light. She was afraid because when she had been alive, she had been bullied by her boyfriend to get rid of the child she was expecting. He had only been thinking of himself and nothing of her or the baby. Under the relentless pressure, she was forced to agree to his wishes. She had been mourning this decision her whole life and now in spirit, she carried it as well. I could hear her crying while the story was being told. This poor deceased girl had felt so much guilt for so long the angels needed help to bring her to them. I pulled the car over to the side of the road and started to pray. The beautiful angel that appeared was of pure white light and the angel was carrying a tiny child, it was the girl's baby. It was a very emotional moment for me. The girl was apprehensive at first, but she eventually moved forward and walked into the light. I was mesmerised by the sheer love and gentleness of the event that had surrounded me. Just as quickly as they had come, they were gone and I was left sitting in my car at the side of the road wiping tears from my eyes. Anyone passing by might have thought I was an emotional basket case. Moments of spirit can happen anywhere and at any time, I just have to be ready to help where and when I can.

Monte just loved the wildness of Donegal and the amazing beaches there. I took him to see Killybegs, Dungloe and Rosbeg that are all in the area. He tried a few pints of Guinness and a traditional hot whiskey, which is great to keep you toasty on a cold winter's day. We went for long walks on beautiful Narin beach and relaxed in front of the fire in the evening. It was getting near to New Year's Eve and we decided to spend the New Year celebrations back in at the cabin. It was great craic most of the family showed up, the furniture was moved out of the way and he got to see some sketchy but passable versions of Irish dancing. Before we knew it, time had flown by and Monte had to return to America.

Having him in Northern Ireland for the holidays had been just wonderful. We got to know so much more about each other's lives, and how different our cultures are. It was the beginning of a new journey in life and love for me. This was to be the start of the two of us traveling, back and forth, between America and Northern Ireland over the next few years, all because I pushed that button on my computer and said hello. I would not see him again for three months and I would miss him terribly, but I had a lot of things to keep me busy between the divorce and annulment, sorting the rest of the house and I had a wall to build and a garden to plant.

Pauline Johnson

CHAPTER 17
Heavenly Lights

It was sad for both of us to say goodbye, but it had to be that way. He had his work to return to and I had things to sort out here as well. I got busy with starting to plan the wall around the garden, and asked my brother Garry to do the job. It would take a bit of time to get it done, but if there was one thing I had, it was time. I also started to arrange to design the garden. It was a bit of a mess and I would have to wait until the wall was done. It was now 2007 and things outside were at last going forward at my home. I would also chat to Monte everyday over video and that was wonderful. The calls were free, which, considering the price of overseas calls, was a huge blessing. I could see him online at home and he could see me. A lot of people would think this unusual for two people trying to have a relationship but we did not mind as long as we got to see each other every day, even if it was on a computer screen. It was making the best of our situation. Sometimes we would literally spent two or three hours chatting, the time would always go so fast. I had arranged to get out to America again at the end of March.

    I was more organised going out to America this time. Even though I had done the trip, I was still nervous and excited to be going back. I had really loved being in Coeur d'Alene. The people and the place had a remarkable quiet energy surrounding it. It was a place to unwind, and loosen up for me. Being there I had done so many things I would never have got the chance to do in Northern Ireland. I had got to shoot bows and arrows, go camping in the wilderness, sword fight, go to farmer's markets and watch concerts in the park on the weekends. The weather was beautiful, and the city was always filled with activities, festivals, and incredible art shops. I would get to see so much more of it this time around. Most of all I had met this wonderful man in this beautiful place. I knew that Heaven must have orchestrated it to be like this. I could never have worked all of these details out so incredibly, there were too many elements that had come together for it to be a coincidence. To think of all the faces I had seen online, that the first one I would say hello to would turn out to be the one I was getting to know. I was not complaining though, I was excited and having some fun for the first time in years. So, I was on my way back to America to stay for another three months.

I arrived late into Spokane airport and Monte was there to pick me up. We were both so glad to see each other it was overwhelming. I did not realise how much I had missed him. He was looking so great and I was glad to have arrived after the gruelling twenty-two hour journey. When we got back to his place, I thought I must have looked such a wreck, but I was too tired to care. The apartment was full of candles, and so cozy and welcoming I fell asleep right away after a wonderful hot shower. I was staying in his beautiful apartment in a quiet area of the city.

It was part of an old house, on the ground floor with a lovely porch to the front and was surrounded with roses, a beautiful garden, and flowering trees. I woke the next morning to the smell of pancakes and coffee. What could be better? We had the next two days together because it was the weekend, so we spent it very quietly after all the travelling. Monday arrived and Monte had to go back to work, but I was going out to visit a few places I had not had the chance to visit before. The weather was mild and perfect for getting out and about so I walked through the neighbourhood, past houses with their flowering gardens, through the little town full of shops and down to the lake. This was how I would spend a lot of my days there.

A few things started to surface that began to cause some minor irritations for us. Everyone has ex-people to deal with at times. It was not something that I was worried about we all have a past of one kind or another and I knew all the details about Monte and his past as he knew about mine. It comes down to the fact of some ex-partners finding it hard to move on and create a new life for themselves. Monte had been single now for quite some time, but occasionally we would cross paths with his past. It also caused difficulty when some of his friends would invite his ex to certain events. I had met her and had not really been bothered if she appeared in our company or not. To me it was in the past, but Monte did not like her being around at all. The band he was in had arranged a night and I was really looking forward to going. Kite was a progressive rock band. Monte was the lead singer and has an incredible voice. It took him a lot of effort to organise and prepare, but the show went off brilliantly. The band had such a polished sound, but then they had spent years touring the country together. The only thing to dampen the evening was the ex-girlfriend, who went up on stage and took the mic to give her thoughts on how great the band was. I wasn't the only one there thinking that her behaviour was a bit strange it was a little confusing to say the least. I did not say anything until I came back to the apartment. We were both annoyed by the time we got home, and it ended up in a bit of an argument. We did see the funny side of it all the next day, but at the time, the strangest thing happened. We were standing in front of a lamp, arguing about how the events had unfolded to do with the evening. When I get annoyed, I use my hands while I am talking. I was in the middle of this when Monte started to look at me and then at the lamp.

He said, "Did you see that?"

I was really frustrated and in the middle of making some point or other, "What?"

He said, "Do that again!"

I realised for the first time he was talking about the lamp. When I put my hand near the lamp, it would go off and when I took my hand away it would come on. All I could think was, this man is not listening to me at all. I said, "The lamp? What about the lamp? You mean this?" I put my hand near to the lamp and the light would go off and come on again when I moved it away. I did not care if the lamp was going on and off at the time. He looked a bit shocked to watch me doing this, but it also ended the argument. The energy I was putting out was affecting the lamp. Monte and I tested it a couple more times, but it stopped working once I had calmed down.

The incident reminded me of the day I had got married, when all the lights in the chapel had gone out as I started to walk up the aisle. I was starting to realise that there was a connection. My energy, if strong enough, would affect the electrical things around me. After the argument, things where back to how they had been. Nothing and no one is perfect in this world. We can all carry baggage from the past and sometimes it interferes with our present. It may feel uncomfortable, but only if we let it affect us in that way. The feeling of adventure and happiness totally out weighted the small annoying moments.

Because I walked most days in Coeur d'Alene, I would pass this bicycle shop on my way through the town. It had the most beautiful hand painted bicycles I had ever seen. One in particular would catch my eye every time I would pass. It was yellow and had a basket holder and a big rear fender that covered the back wheel with bright red tulips hand painted all over. These bikes were old fashioned, styled with the modern twists. I had seen similar bikes in Amsterdam when I had visited there a few years previously. I stopped to have a better look at this beautiful bike. Then I decided I would call back and bring Monte with me to see it. When we called back I already decided it was mine. He thought it would be great as well, especially to get around the local area. It would also help me to get used to the road systems in America. Sometimes even crossing the road was dangerous for me because I always had the tendency to look in the wrong direction first. I am used to driving with the steering wheel on the right side of a car and the left side of the road. It can be a bit confusing. I thought that the bike would be a good start. Completely excited, I rode the bike back to the apartment, laughing like a kid again. When Monte got back from work, we decided to go out for a bit to get used to the roads. He was sorting his own bike at this time and it was in a shop that was a short distance from the apartment so he jogged along beside me. As I cycled down this road amongst all the trees, the most beautiful huge yellow-orange butterfly flew along beside me for most of the way. Butterflies in my cards mean transformation, I thought how appropriate it was, I had not been out cycling like this since

I was a child. It was a time of huge transformation for me in every way to say the least.

Monte had seen the butterfly as well. He said it looked so comical with it flying beside me all the way like a pet, and it matched the yellow of my bicycle perfectly. He explained that the butterfly was called a Monarch, and common in Idaho. Because of its beauty it is considered the king of the butterflies hence the name Monarch. I had never seen a butterfly that big and majestic before, but I always think of the angels when I see them. I looked at it as a sign from the angels that they were close by and looking after me. The next day we went to pick up Monte's bike.

I was so excited the next morning and that childlike feeling was still with me. I was looking forward to be out and about and having my own wheels. I think it made me feel more at home to have a bicycle parked outside the apartment. We had breakfast and again with Monte walking and me on my bike we set off for the bike shop. They have cycle lanes in Coeur d'Alene, but the tree roots make it awkward to cycle on them. At times I would have to be on the pavement and cycle through parking lots to get around the problem. We were in a busy section of the town, nearing the bike shop to pick up Monte's bike. The shop was on a corner at a crossroads, and a car accident had occurred just as we were arriving. I was about a hundred yards a head of Monte and about ten feet from the end of the road. There were queues of traffic at each of the four lanes at the crossroads waiting on the police to clear the accident. Just as I was pulling up to stop I saw a young woman, impatient with waiting, pull out and cut across the corner of the parking lot, heading straight for me. Everything slowed down around me. Suddenly the sky came alive with thousands of sparkling lights. I forgot about the car, all I could do was stare in wonder at the lights coming down around me from the sky. I could not take my gaze from them they were so beautiful. They completely surrounded me like a shower and after what seemed like several minutes, though it was probably more like seconds, I could hear Monte calling out behind me, he sounding so worried. In a blink the sparkling lights where gone and Monte caught up to me, "That woman in the car nearly hit you! Are you alright? You need to stay closer to me on that bike until you get used to the streets, and what were you looking up at in the sky, did you not see her?"

I replied, "Did you see the lights all around me, they where incredible!"

He didn't know what to say. He had just seen me riding my bike, staring at the sky while some crazy woman almost ran me over. I was so mesmerised by what I was watching I just knew that the woman was not meant to hit me. Monte said she had swerved around me, but it must have been so close, he was shaken by it. I felt totally fine and not at all scared. I have no idea if the lights were the angels, my spirit guides, or other realms, but I do know I was completely protected in that light while it was going on. It was like each light had a rainbow inside it and there where thousands of them. It left me with a heavenly surreal feeling I was so blessed to experience it. Monte knew I was looking at something when I stopped the bike, and that it was real enough to stop me looking at the car speeding toward me. He had not seen the lights, but he did say something had kept me safe from being badly injured that day.

We eventually got across the street and got his bicycle. I asked Monte after this event, how he felt about being around me and about the things that can happen sometimes. He said it was all very new to him, at first a bit scary, but that he was getting more used to it. I had seen the way he would look at me sometimes and I needed to know he was ok with it all. I think humour was important for both of us, to be able to see the lighter side of the unusual things that had happened is a good alternative to freaking out. Over the next few months, we would go out cycling to all kinds of places. I bought a basket for the front of the bike and Monte painted it bright red to match the tulips. Now I was able to carry groceries and small items back home when I was out. I loved seeing their massive stores and the different kinds of food available. We both love to cook so it was fun to do all of these things together. I was having a ball.

I do know it would not suit everyone to have a relationship in this way, being six thousand miles apart and having to travel and leave after ninety days, but it was great for me at the time. I had nothing to tie me in Ireland

and was able to be away for three months at a time if I chose to be. It was a breath of fresh air to be in this part of the world. I had so much time to myself and it gave me the ability to look at my situation from a distance and gain fresh perspective.

Monte would go to work and I could go and explore the art shops and galleries in the town. Our relationship was growing and we were very happy together but we were still taking it slowly. I would be returning home to Northern Ireland soon. Ninety days is all I am allowed when visiting America, so it was time to get ready to leave again. It was the end of May and we would not be able to see each other again until September. I think being apart for these months helped us to get closer in a way, but it also gave us space to have our independence and ease into our relationship. I had learned from the past that getting lost in another person's life is detrimental to your mind, body and soul. It is so much more spiritually, emotionally, and physically healthy to have your own independence and presence as a person while still being open to love and be loved. Being an emotional crutch for the person you love, or allowing the person you care for to be overly needy, will always create problems that will escalate as it goes on. Another person cannot make you happy inside; you must do that for yourself. Being dependent on Monte for my happiness or anything else was something I did not want for this relationship. It was good to have the feeling of freedom between us and not expectation, it reminded me of the story of Jane.

When Jane came to me she arrived like a whirlwind. She had brought such wonderful energy with her and a smile that just made me feel so at ease in her company. Her energy was uplifting and strong until she talked about love relationships in her life. Then you could actually feel the difference in her total character. Jane is a counsellor, but had issues in love relationships. She was having difficulty leaving a relationship behind while starting a new one that had its own problems. She had been in an unhealthy relationship for a number of years and had lost her self-esteem and self-worth somewhere in the middle of it all. Her new relationship wasn't much better. The one thing she did have was a male friend that thought the world of her and was always trying to help. It may sound like a very confusing position to be in but sometimes we are being shown in no uncertain terms what we need to do, we just have to find the strength to do it. That day the angels came in very clearly and let Jane know that her life would eventually change. Her visit to me showed her that she would be taking an important trip related to her work. I was told to tell her that she would be going to Canada. She knew nothing about any journey. "Me? I am not going anywhere Pauline." She told me shaking her head. The angels also let her know that the issues about her old relationship would be resolved in a good way, but that she had to have patience. So often it is the message of patience that comes through. We all want change but no one wants to wait or work for it. God is seldom about overnight solutions I think.

While I am with a person sometimes I will start to call the person I have in front of me by another name. At first I thought it was because I needed to be more grounded and focused. This started to happen to me for the first time when I had the visit from Jane. Every time I wanted to say Jane, the name 'Fiona' would come into the front of my mind in the same place where words go to wait before being spoken. The impression was so strong that I called Jane 'Fiona' two times before I caught myself. Both times I laughed and apologised but then I received a strong message and had to ask Jane, "I have wanted to call you Fiona so many times while we have been sitting here I just have to ask: Is there a time you where to be called Fiona or have a family member deceased called Fiona?" She just flushed and told me that she had been to another lady that had an angel connection where she had learned that her guardian angel's name was Fiona. Well that was a new one for me and it explained the experience I was getting at the same time. This same thing has happened so often now that I recognise that it's the person's guardian angel introducing themselves. It was a great confirmation for Jane that her guardian angel was there guiding her.

The angels told Jane that she would see changes start to happen quite soon, but also it has to be in accordance with Divine timing and not to her own. Her message was very clear and positive. The good male friend she had was showing her what qualities she should be looking for in a male companion. She had been so badly treated for such a long time in the relationships she had been in that it was what Jane had come to see as normal. But she learned to see that, far from normal, the relationships had been abusive and damaging. I heard from Jane about nine months later when she came back to me for another visit. She had indeed been to Canada and it had been an amazing trip for her, she was there for three months. She said she was more than a bit shocked when it had come about, as it was totally unplanned. Because she was away from her situation for the three months it helped her distance herself and see what it would feel like to be free from the relationships. The old relationship worries had also moved on but she had to make up her mind about the relationship she was still involved in. She was so much happier within herself and I think she is on a better road and to making good choices for her life. Again, the angels of God's love and light will always help us. We just have to invite them in and thank them when they do.

Love without restraints is free to grow and bloom. When two people say they love each other, sometimes you find one will try to make the relationship all about them. That is called control or it can be just plain selfishness or they expect them to give up all their own interests and only have theirs. Each person was not put on this earth to pander to another person's whims or demands just because they are in a love relationship. Neither do they have to put up with any aggressive behaviour from a loved one, or listen to words that are critical or hurtful in any way over and over. Should it happen because of alcohol, drugs, gambling or anything else does not matter. Everyone is individual, truly unique and beautiful just as they are. True love of another person will always be mindful of this fact. My favourite bible verse clearly explains love to us:

A Heavenly Gift

[1 Corinthians 13:4-7]

Love is patient, love is kind.
It does not envy, it does not boast, it is not proud.
It does not dishonour others, it is not self-seeking,
It is not easily angered, it keeps no record of wrong doing.
Love does not delight in evil but rejoices with the truth.
It always protects, always trusts,
Always hopes, always perseveres.
Love never fails.

This beautiful verse is a guideline for us in this day and age, if we feel confused in a love relationship. I have read this verse so often to help me see more clearly, what is right and good. I know that I deserve the finest and truest love for my heart. If it contradicts with the words in this verse, then I need to take a good look at what is really going on. Relationships can pull us in so many different directions, being flexible is normal, but being constantly weighted down in a relationship is definitely not. This new relationship for me was just starting and it felt light and happy.

Thinking of being back in Northern Ireland, I knew the wall around the garden would be well on the way. I had talked to my brother Garry on the phone several times and knew he was working hard to get the wall built. It was going to be so lovely to get the garden started and growing, so I was excited about going home and I knew the months would fly by. I would be keeping myself busy and so would Monte. We both did not like the thought of the goodbyes at the airport, but it couldn't be helped. My trip back to America had been really wonderful and I had got to know a great deal more about Idaho and about Monte.

A Heavenly Gift

Pauline Johnson

CHAPTER 18
Wandering & Windows

Garry picked me up at the Dublin airport and we got on the road home. I was tired a little sad, but happy when I thought of all the new things that were ahead for me. When I arrived home I called in to visit my mum and gave her a hug, chatted for a little while and then went straight to my bed. I woke the next day in the afternoon; my internal clock was all over the place yet again. When Garry came around to trail me outside, I was so happy to see the wall was very much underway. Of course I got the usual jokes said to me that I was building the great wall of Ballygawley and when was I going to be posting the guards. It was funny, but I had my own ideas for how I wanted the outside of my log cabin to look and I was sticking to that. I missed Monte, but time was already flying by. I had arranged to have a landscape company come out and start the garden, but the weather was so wet it was put on hold for a bit. It was okay I had other more important things that were finally coming to an end. I had been waiting on the result of annulments and divorce details. As I have explained earlier, because I am a Catholic, both the divorce and the annulment are required in order for me to be free to move forward. After years of waiting, driving back and forth to Belfast and having legal confrontations over and over, the divorce was now finalised. It was strange event because it only took ten minutes to be legally binding after nearly fifteen years of marriage. It had taken a further eight years since we had separated for it to be finished. It was the final sad and necessary step to letting go of the past. It was not so easy to let the past go and I had spent so much time dwelling on it but it had taken so many years already. This happened at the end of June and I had already made travel plans to go back to Coeur d'Alene in September.

Over the next two months, I was involved with my niece's wedding. I was the photographer and had to make sure all the pictures came out great. It turned out to be a wonderful day and I really enjoyed doing the photos. Monte had been invited but couldn't get the time off of work to come. I was excited to be seeing him again I had really missed him over the last three months. Of course, we talked every day, but it was not the same as being in the same place together. He was really excited that I was soon on my way back to America and that I would be there for Halloween, Thanksgiving and my birthday this time.

As the ground fell away out of Dublin, I was so happy to be getting to return to Coeur d'Alene. I wasn't thinking of the long trip or all the airports I would be going through, I knew the route very well this time around. Finally I arrived and got wrapped up in a big hug at the bottom of the stairs in Spokane Airport. It was such a wonderful warm feeling to be back together. As usual, I was exhilarated to be there, but completely knackered. We had so much to chat about and catch up on, but we just ended up laughing out of the sheer joy of being reunited. At least this time when a place or name was mentioned I knew who it was and where it was. It was like a home away from home for me. He had the apartment looking beautiful and cozy. I would appreciate it more the next day though when I had a good rest.

Getting up the next day, the sun was shining and there was my yellow bike parked outside all ready to go. He had got some new porch furniture and told me to watch out for the hummingbirds that gathered at the feeders hanging outside. Once again the stunning natural beauty of North Idaho brought new delights to me. We don't have hummingbirds in Ireland which is sad because they are so busy and beautiful. It was the first time I had seen one. They are amazingly colourful and quick in their movements. I could have watched them for hours and never got bored. We went out that day on Monte's motorbike and went to see some wolves. Wolf People is a family business that looks after sick or injured wolves from the wild. I was shocked at the size some of the adult wolves, some of them were as big as my sofa! The people took us into the back area where a wolf pup lay panting in the heat. He was about the size of an adult German Shepherd. His coat was white and grey and he was very relaxed, we even got to pet him. It was so fascinating. On the way, we passed a huge herd of American Buffalo. It really gave me a feel for the old west.

I was seated behind Monte on his motorcycle as we cruised through the mountains and I told him that I wondered what Buffalo tasted like. On the way home that evening we stopped into a local butcher and picked up two massive buffalo steaks. When we got back he put the steaks on the barbecue, they were fantastic. It was a time to see and experience more of America.

I was there about three weeks this time when Monte said we were going on a trip to see Seattle and the San Juan Islands. I was thrilled to be going to see these places. The San Juan Islands are where the Orca and Humpback whales migrate on their way to Alaska, so we were really hoping to see them. We went to Seattle first and then to the islands. In the middle of all this there was also one of the historical sword fighting tournaments that Monte would participate in, though it was more hysterical than historical I always thought. We all need a good laugh every so often and that is what these were like to watch. The group would really get into it, with the swords and the outfits. The band of course was another part of his life. I have always loved music and being in a band in the past myself I fitted right into it all. Montes other band members were all married and had known each other for years, they all lived in close proximity to each other. One of them lived down the street from Monte's apartment. I got on with them all really well and we had visited each of their houses at different times for dinner.

His friend and band member Jim lived close by and had us over one particular evening. We were all out in the garden at Jim's house and it was getting a bit colder because it was now autumn in Idaho. People spend a lot of time in their gardens in that part of the world, sitting around wood fires in the evenings. When I said I was cold Monte left and brought me back a fleece to keep me warm. I put it on and later when the evening was ending, we said our goodbyes and headed home. It was a bit chilly in the apartment so I decided to wear the fleece over my pyjamas. It was early when I went to bed and, falling asleep, I started to dream so vividly. In my dream I was back at Jim's house and I was trying to light the fire in the fireplace in their house. I was striking matches, but they were being blown out and I could see my breath. In the dream, I turned to a window on the right and I could see a hand and hear this knocking on the window. I knew the hand was female and she knocked three times. I started to walk down the hall, I knew in the dream I had to wake Jim and his wife, something was wrong and they needed to know about it. I suddenly woke and sat up in the bed in the apartment. The time on the clock was twelve twenty six. It was such a strong dream, I had to wake Monte and I explained about the dream. I told him that I thought there was something very wrong at his friend's house. I was so flustered and overheating having slept in the fleece. "Your fleece is too warm." I said taking it off. He replied, "That's not my fleece, it's one of Jim's." I took it off then, but the unease was still there and I was convinced something was not right. Monte said, "It was just a dream Pauline, don't worry." I relaxed a little then and went back to bed.

The next morning I woke, thinking of my dream but not really bothered by it. I went out to sit on the porch at the front of the apartment, it was a beautiful sunny morning and I looked down the street to where Jim and his wife lived. Jim's car was just pulling out from their house and heading in my direction. Monte had come out of the house at this time and Jim stopped. I thought it was just to say hello, so I went over. I said, "Hi Jim, how are you, I had the strangest dream about you and being in your house last night." I told him how I thought something bad had happened and that I wanted to call to wake him and tell him about it, but it was too late to call when it happened at twelve twenty six. I was laughing it all off, but Jim was looking at me and seemed to be a little shocked.

He replied, "My grandmother died last night at around twelve thirty."

He was close to his grandmother and he was certainly not expecting to hear such a story this morning. He looked at me again and then drove off to his parent's house to organise the details of the funeral. His grandmother's funeral was held two days after this. She had come from Ireland and Jim had always wanted to visit Ireland where she had been living while growing up. It was strange how I had received this dream about needing to tell people that I had only met, that something bad had happened. I had experienced the window being knocked in this way before in Northern Ireland when a person close to me had died. It was like their way of saying that they were leaving and to say goodbye. Death brings such sadness but a beautiful new beginning for the person's soul to carry on in the light with all the people that are close to them in spirit and the Angels.

    Dreams have guided me at other times in my life, sometimes it can be the only way your guardian angel can get through if you have a lot going on, or your mind is full of worry. I have had dreams warning me of things that are coming up in the future and dreams about others close to me. I had a particular dream one night; I was in an old house and I was sitting beside a priest on a sofa having a conversation. The priest was telling me that he had lived in the house before he died and I could also see the relatives of a friend in the same room. A little girl was skipping about and she came to me and told me that one of the people there had really bad depression. When the dream ended I really wanted to know more details about what I had been shown. I contacted a friend that knew the family I had seen and asked him about the house in the dream. He was surprised when I described the detail of the house inside, but more so when I told him that a priest had lived in the house before the people that were living there now. It turned out to all be correct, a priest had lived there previously and the sitting room was exactly how I described it. The family who now lived there had lost a little girl who used to skip about the house and her older sister was very depressed at her passing. I relayed the message to the person that needed to know about it and that is all I was asked to do. I learned later that it helped the family involved to be more aware of how depressed their daughter was and to get her some help.

    Another dream I was given was a message from my father. I heard his voice so clearly after the dream that I completely woke up. He showed me someone trying to hide letters from me and told me to check all paperwork carefully. I had been dealing with so much paperwork at the time that I could not pinpoint what letter this could be. But after the dream from him I was much more cautious. It turned out that while I had to gather requested information it seemed that not all the relevant documents were being disclosed from the other party involved. I got more solid validation about all this shortly after the dream from my dad. Sometimes I also get flash dreams or dreams that contain more symbols than a straight forward message, these can be harder to understand at the time, but when I trust my own intuition I am usually spot on with the meaning for me.

    In everyone's life are unending cycles of endings and beginnings. My annulment also came up at this time, it had been five long years to complete I had no way of knowing if it would be granted. I was so relieved when I was got the legal document to tell me I had been given my annulment. Now I was free to get on with my life. It was a quiet thankfulness, as there is also a great sadness attached to these events. I did hope that my ex-husband was now much happier that these things had been sorted.

    Monte and I got packed for the trip to Seattle shortly after Jim's granny had died. It was an eight hour road trip through the plains of Eastern Washington, then over the mountains through the Snoqualmie Pass and finally to the coast. The scenery was beautiful and always changing. The American highways are vast. We stayed right in the centre of the city and visited places I had only seen on TV. We went up to the top of the Space Needle and the views over Seattle were spectacular. We then headed to the Museum of Pop Culture and had a look at all the relics of American rock and roll. As it was the first day we took it a little easy, but the following day we went to the Pikes Place market, famous for the wonderful crafts, chocolate and coffee shops and the vendors that throw fish to each other, it is so comical. Then we went on to the Seattle Aquarium, one of my favourite places to see. It's at Pier 59 and we got to touch and explore some of the most exciting creatures. The starfish in the huge tanks were like no starfish I had ever seen. They were massive and were all different colours and the variety of fish were so beautiful. It was a truly fascinating trip. We left Seattle the next day and headed to the San Juan Islands.

We had to go across to Friday Harbour by ferry and the boat trip took about an hour. Seeing the islands from the boat was amazing, and it was such a calm boat trip. When we arrived, I laughed because right on the harbour was an Irish pub. We checked it out after we got booked into a beautiful house overlooking the sea. The San Juan Islands are a very romantic place to be. It was quiet because it was late in the season, but there were still plenty of people about. We spent the rest of the day and evening exploring the town and sorting out a boat trip to go and see the whales in the morning. I was thrilled to be getting the chance to see them. It wasn't guaranteed, but there was a possibility they might be in the area. As it turned out, we did not see any, but we did get to see porpoises, seals and eagles and so much more of the islands. We went through Portland, Oregon on the way back.

It had been a busy week so far and going to Portland down the coast was really dramatic. It has a very rugged coastline, a bit like the coast of Donegal, but more forested. We stayed outside Portland in a cozy house at the sea it was a great end to a fascinating trip. We were totally worn out by the time we got back, but it was worth it. I had got to see places and meet people that were truly wonderful.

October was arriving and we went out for a day to pick pumpkins. I had never seen so many pumpkin fields in my life. They came in all shapes, sizes and colours. It was great fun to be in the middle of all the Halloween preparations. In America they seem to make so much more of a celebration of the seasons, and more of an effort to bring people together to enjoy it all. There was a real festival atmosphere to the whole day, with music, mulled wine and all kinds of food from the local farmers in the area. We took two of the biggest pumpkins home with us to carve and put on the front porch, which was another new event for me, I felt like a child again. I recommend everyone to have a go at it no matter what age. My birthday was also coming up and it was nice to be together for that.

A Heavenly Gift

We spent my birthday going for a walk and having dinner later on, it was quiet and fun. Thanksgiving arrived at the end of November. It is just like Christmas day in Ireland. They cook a turkey dinner and have the whole family together. I got to meet Monte's brother and his wife around this time they are a wonderful couple. Both are very talented musically and it was great to get to meet up and spend some time with them. Monte and I were much more relaxed as a couple by now and we really enjoyed doing the same things. His friend Jim invited us to a party at his house for the sword fighting group after Thanksgiving. We sat outside around the fire and watched the swashbuckling. While I was watching Monte in one of his bouts, I sensed a change in the energy. It's hard to explain, it's like I lost the feeling of lightness in the air. I looked around and then across the garden at the small building Jim used for an office. At the door I saw a black figure the height, shape and size of a man walking from the door. I can only describe it like a shadow, but completely black. It was another first for me. I had never seen anything in that form before that day. It just faded away as it walked.

At the same time I saw the figure, Monte pulled a muscle in his leg and we ended up going back to the apartment. I was glad we left early because it was unnerving to see something that dark around some of Monte's friends. The shadow I was allowed to see was shown to me for some good reason, but I do not know exactly why or who it was attaching itself to. I do know it was not a good energy.

I mentioned before about all the art galleries in the middle of Coeur d'Alene. One in particular had the most beautiful stained glass for sale. The windows were created by a local lady who created the most wonderful designs of angels. I loved to go into the shop in the morning when the windows would catch the sun coming in. When I called in one morning, a new stained glass piece had arrived. It was one of the most beautiful angel pieces in the shop, the colours were deep red, pink, blues, greens and the belt around her middle held a crystal that sparkled rays of light when the sun shone. The outside frame of glass that surrounded it had all the colours of the rainbow. It was so special and I knew from the moment I set eyes on it that it would be mine. I didn't buy it right away, as I had no idea where I would put it or how I would get it to Ireland. I continued to walk past the shop window for another few days before I finally went in and bought it.

I was going home again in three days so I sorted out the angel window to be shipped before I left. The stained glass angel was large, about three and a half feet high and two and a half feet wide. I thought it would be at least fourteen days for a fragile piece like that to arrive in Northern Ireland and hoped it would not be in bits when it got there. I was packing my cases for the return journey two days later when my phone rang. It was my mum calling to tell me that a large parcel had arrived for me and she had no idea what it was. I couldn't believe it got there so quickly. I joked with my mum that it must have flown all the way there itself. When we unwrapped it at home in Northern Ireland it was perfect. I arrived home again two days later and Monte was coming for Christmas again on the nineteenth of December. I only had three weeks to wait until Monte joined me again in Northern Ireland. When I got home, I was surprised and pleased to see the pond started in my garden and the wall finished. It was still pretty mucky and untidy but it would be lovely when it was finished. I took my new stained glass angel into the cabin and left it in its box. I still didn't know where I was going to put it, but that would be made clearer in the New Year. I had been doing some psychic work when I was at home, but travelling back and forth to America made it hard to build a client base. It was something I really did want to get sorted. I had not thought I would end up spending so much time in America. I also had to start thinking about starting to sort out my livelihood.

A Heavenly Gift

Pauline Johnson

CHAPTER 19

Heavenly Havens

Christmas together was wonderful and Monte returned to Idaho on the seventh of January, but in the beginning of April I would follow him. We missed each other more than ever, but again, it couldn't be helped. The gardeners had been back and were putting in plants and some trees outside the cabin and making the garden look a lot more normal. The small lawn area was just clay, but it was ready for planting and would be much greener by summer. I was looking forward to it being done and finished. There was so much that had happened over the past few years. I was back in a relationship and I had not expected to be in such a good one, even though it was a very long distance one. I had lots of other things to be getting on with after Monte left and I really enjoyed the time I had to myself as well. I now had my own small, but beautiful log cabin my garden was coming together and it was time to be sorting a place to do my spiritual work. I had decided to add a small room to the front of the cabin where the porch was. It would not be very big, but it was perfect for what I needed it for. I was not going to have it done until I came back from America in June.

I had also decided that when I was in America I wanted to go to a sixth sensory course in Chicago. I had read about the course and really wanted to meet some people with similar stories and backgrounds. I was excited to be getting the chance to learn how others did their work and what their experiences were. I was back in America for three weeks when I went to Chicago. There where about a hundred people there for the same course. It was only on for three days and it was done in a relaxed fun way. I got to meet so many wonderful people from all over the world. There were people there from Canada, El Salvador, Brazil,

A Heavenly Gift

England, Iceland and of course, America. It was an eye opener for me to get a chance to talk to these people about their gifts and how they were using them to help others. There was quite an array of professions represented including, teachers, lawyers, social workers, and psychics. These were people with intuitive gifts and they were using them to get to the truth of so many different situations to help and heal other people. I am still in touch with most of these people and they are truly inspiring. I was glad that I had gone to the six sensory course it stretched my perceptions of what is possible when you follow your instincts. One part of the course was to read other people energy. I had no expectations about what would happen so I was totally open to have a go.

    We were paired together and I sat in front of this lovely woman named Liz. She told me that she was nervous and I replied, "Good, because I am as well." Admitting it relaxed us both immediately. As the exercise started I closed my eyes and asked Serena to help me. Suddenly I saw an array of colours forming an outline of her in front of me. It was very clear even though I still had my eyes closed. There was one bit of bright red light and another darker mark beside it standing out from all the other areas of her body. I brought all my focus to that spot and then I opened my eyes. The first thing I saw when I opened my eyes was that, Liz had two Native Americans behind her. They looked like a grandfather and grandmother with feather headdresses. At first the image of them was very vivid and then slowly, they faded. I was a bit shocked to say the least. Coming from Northern Ireland I had never seen a true Native American, but I was also ecstatic to have connected so clearly. I told her, "Liz you were just surrounded by Native American Indians. Does that make sense to you?"

She smiled and said, "Yes, my grandparents were Native Americans."

Then I asked her about the bright red light I had seen around the area of her heart. I asked her if she had recent illness or anything in the past that had damaged her heart in any way. She was a little surprised and I explained that I had seen two marks on her heart. One looked like it had healed and the other mark still looked raw and needed more healing. She told me of the two heartbreaks she had suffered in her life. The first was from the death of her husband some years previously and the second was from a break up with her partner after being together for a several years. She told me that both of these events had left her with a deep and painful ache in her heart. She was shocked that I had seen this, and I have to say I was a little shocked myself at the time, but I was thankful for being able to talk to her about it. Sometimes just sharing and talking about our problems or sadness to another person is very healing. It can be overwhelming to be shown such powerful emotional insights into people's lives. I thanked Liz for being so open and relaxed with me. The course was a learning experience for me in more ways than one. I also learned that there are some practices that just aren't for me. Liz's reading was one of the highlights of the trip.

I was back in Coeur d'Alene with Monte after the course and we were just sitting chatting on his porch as we did most evenings. We talked about the course and about faith and God, and then we started to talk about Our Lady and the angels.

Monte turned to me and said, "Do you smell roses?"

At first, I could not smell anything, but then it got so strong I couldn't mistake it for anything else. It all seemed to surround Monte more than me. A gentle beautiful warmth came along with the scent. We both had no doubt that with the scent of roses it was Our Lady sending us a little glimpse of the love and warmth that she gives. There where rose bushes around the apartment but not in bloom at this time. Monte was in the process of becoming a Catholic. It is not something I had been pushing on him or telling him about, this was something he was looking into all on his own and had begun before we met. Because I am from Northern Ireland it was not something that came to my mind very often, most people I knew are born into it. Monte would ask me at different times about certain things to do with it all. I would tell him everyone may have a different opinion about what it is, but the way I look at it is that God does not change, only people's attitudes and thoughts change. It is the one thing in my life that stays the same, no matter what. When I have no one to turn to, God, Jesus, Mary, and His angels and saints are always there for me. It is not something I preach about to anyone. My relationship with God is a very personal thing, a relationship that is love, gentleness and beauty. It was something that would grow for Monte, and I would get to experience a wonderful event later that I had never seen before, but the time had come again to go back home. My time in America was always over too quickly, and the more time we spent together the faster it went. I wouldn't see him again until September, it would be three months of waiting and was so hard to say goodbye.

  I came home to a new green lawn and a pond full of water it was really lovely. As usual, I was too tired to take it in when I arrived. There were a lot of things being done while I had been away. I did not have a proper kitchen in my cabin when I left so I had Garry my brother sort one out for me while I was away. It wasn't a fancy kitchen, but I was so pleased that I at least had one. The cabin had to be reorganised, but I get a lot of pleasure from working on the house anyway. I had the whole cabin cleaned and sorted later that day then I just sat down and looked around, it was really coming together now. It was time to focus on adding the room to the front of the house that I needed. I contacted Wildwood Log Cabins again and had Dean the owner call to assess the situation. It had taken a few years to get certain things done, but I had to keep within my budget. When Dean came out I found that it was much easier to add the extra room than I had expected, so I gave him the go ahead. It seemed to me that I was always doing something or going somewhere, but this was the time to be doing things, not sitting and thinking. Dean would not be able to get started until September, but that was fine with me. I decided I wanted the stained glass angel to be the main feature of the room to do my spiritual work and made arrangements with Dean to install it, it just seemed the perfect place for it to be.

Soon three months had flown by, and Monte was on his way to Ireland. We had been keeping in contact every day over Skype but it wasn't again the same as hugging him and being in his presence. We were so happy to see each other it made all the time apart worth it. He was jet lagged for the first week, but then he was ready to be on the move again. The work to the front room was being done and the gardeners were still doing their finishing touches. I'm not sure how the conversation came up about going to Lourdes in France, but it was something we both wanted to do.

Lourdes it a very special place of pilgrimage in the world some people are of the opinion that it is too commercialised and all the souvenir shops take away from the experience. I knew I had to go and see for myself what it was like and not to let hearsay dictate my opinion. So Monte and I were off again.

The story of Lourdes: In 1858 in the grotto of Massabielle, the Blessed Virgin Mary appeared eighteen times to Bernadette Soubirous. She was a fourteen-year-old peasant girl. Our Lady identified herself to Bernadette as the Immaculate Conception and she gave Bernadette a message for the world, to pray and do penance for the conversion of the world. All of this was investigated for four years by the civil authorities at that time, they attempted to force her to retract her accounts, but she refused and word quickly spread about the visions and the healing spring that had appeared. Bernadette later became

Saint Bernadette of Lourdes, and a film was made called The Song of Bernadette. Lourdes has since become one of the most famous shrines to Our Lady, attracting more than a million pilgrims each year. Thousands of miraculous cures at the shrine have happened. The cures that take place there have been verified by a group of doctors that include both believers and non-believers, this is still the practice today. Lourdes gives us a gift and no one leaves without a gain in faith. The cures in a moral or spiritual way are marvellous for everyone, not just the physical ones. It is one of the heavenly havens in this world that gives peace, healing and light to all who visit.

    We went for three days, it was a short trip, but we were excited to be going. We had to go by London and then on to Paris, we had just arrived in Lourdes when one of the processions had started. We could see the procession heading past our hotel and everyone was holding candles and singing, it was a beautiful sight. I had heard about what goes on in Lourdes, but as usual, it is totally different when you are standing right there. We put our stuff into the hotel and went back outside and followed everyone else. The pilgrims were in the thousands it was an amazing sight. We enjoyed Lourdes it is truly beautiful not only for the divine atmosphere, but for the town as well. It had some wonderful restaurants and shops. Three days whirled by and soon we were on our way back home.

When we got back we discovered that Dean was nearly finished adding the extra room. The stained glass window of the angel had been installed and was the first thing that greeted us as we pulled in. Over the next three days, the crew finished up. When it was done I was over the moon, the little room was perfect! My own heavenly haven to do my work was finished at last. Monte and I were going back to America for a while and then returning again at Christmas. The trips back and forth, though no easier, had become routine. It was nice this time that we would be travelling together. Coeur d'Alene was like a second home for me and I was really happy to be there. I did realise that I would have to eventually get grounded at home to start building up my spiritual work to attract more people. For now, I was fine with being away, but I also trusted that God had a plan for me and I did not mind waiting for everything to fall into place.

We were so happy to be together. Meeting each other so quickly in such an unusual way was surprising enough, but the way that we clicked was even more rare. Loving after you feel you have failed miserably can be so hard. Letting myself feel vulnerable and trusting again seemed at times like trying to eat Mount Everest with a bendy spoon. The deeper you get involved, the bigger the doubts and worry can appear. I think we were both taking it gently and not really expecting too much too soon. We had been together for a few years, but it still seemed like such a short time. Spending three months apart at a time helped in some ways but didn't in others. The longer we were together, the more we wanted to stay together, but we did not have the luxury of that. It is ironic at times there are always things in life that have to be a certain way for them to work and this was one of those times.

I had worked to create a life in Northern Ireland and Monte had worked to create a life in America. It was something we would be dealing with for a while to come.

Monte had some changes happening around him as well, he got a new job for a different company that was really great for him. He started his new job when we arrived back to America. He was working for a good company and he had been promoted to Marketing Director. His band wasn't doing so well and after many years together they parted ways. Being a wonderful singer and musician he has written so many incredible songs and music, it was sad to watch his talent become so stagnant in his band. But sometimes it's better to let something go if little good is coming from it. I was glad to be there for him at this time and I knew he would make the right decision about what he wanted to do.

  We again enjoyed the Halloween, Thanksgiving and birthday celebrations together. Before we could return to Northern Ireland, winter came to Idaho. In that part of the country it snows a lot. Temperatures are usually below zero and winter can last up to six months or more. Usually in Coeur d'Alene they would have six or seven feet of snow on higher ground. On the day before our return to Ireland, it started to snow heavily. The storm got so bad that Monte decided we should go and stay at a hotel that night to be near to the airport to be able to be on time. I did not like the thought of driving in the snowy conditions, but the white stuff was accumulating even as I watched out the window. We had to move fast or we wouldn't be going anywhere. It only took minutes for us to load Monte's truck and get onto the highway. No one was on the road except for the snow-plows. It was post-apocalyptic. Monte drove the truck through high drifts and we couldn't even see the road, but amazingly we reached the hotel. The front desk clerk couldn't believe that people were actually walking through the front door. The next morning revealed that over three feet of snow had fallen overnight. It was a record setting storm and it was still coming down. When we arrived at the airport, we discovered that all the flights had been cancelled. It would be impossible to make all of our connections in time, but we told the girl at the desk we would fly to anywhere and try to get connections as we went. To add to the chaos, it was only five days before Christmas and the airport was packed. I thought, A*ngels, if ever we need help, it's now!* Just as I prayed this, the girl, out of all the people waiting, singled us out and told us there was one plane leaving Spokane right at that moment. It was the last plane out and it was only carrying one hundred people and she had found seats for us. I was speechless, and overcome with gratitude to God and his angels. We quickly scrambled out to the plane and buckled into our seats, stunned to be there at all. We were flying to Oregon instead of Chicago, but we didn't mind, we could make our way once we got out of the storm. Being flexible had been the major factor in the ticket attendant's ability to help us. It would make the journey back much longer, but at least we were together and making our way home. The journey ended up being one of the most rushed trips I have ever had. We practically ran though airports to catch our connecting flights. It took over thirty hours of travel to get home. We sat in the cabin that next evening watching the news about the storm and having a cup of tea by the fire. We thought again how blessed we had been through the whole trip. Even today, we marvel at how we managed to get home.

Pauline Johnson

CHAPTER 20

Baptism & Birth

The new room needed painting and we had to stain shelves and buy furniture. Christmas was drawing to an end and I had planned to finish off the room when Monte went back to America. We wanted to be able to be together all the time now - it was not easy living in two different countries. I do not think it would suit everyone, but when it comes to love, sometimes the hardships make us try all that much harder to make it work. He headed back to his life and work and I got on with advertising my work. Monte said he would design a logo for my spiritual work. I had no idea what name to give the business; I didn't really think of it as a business, it was more of a calling.

In the end, he set up a web site for me called www.Angelwoodhouse.com it was so appropriate because of the log cabin and the beautiful angel window at the front of the building. I thought the web site looked great and at least it would be there for people to read about what I did and book appointments. I call the angel in the beautiful room window 'Grace'.

One of the first people in the newly unfinished room was with a lovely man named Pat. I get more men coming to me now than I did at the start and I am glad that they do. Pat had two jobs, one of which was farming though he considered the farming as more of a hobby than a job. It is what he would have loved to be doing all the time. Pat had just split up with his wife and it was very hard on him. He was skeptical to say the least, when he arrived. He did not say very much as he sat down in front of me. When the session started and I mentioned about his marital problems and what was going on with his farm, he started to shake his head. I stopped then and asked him if was he all right.

He looked at me like I was up to something, "Do you know me?"

He asked. I replied, "No, I have no idea who you are, I don't even know your surname and I don't need to."

He shook his head again, cracked a smile and said, "So far all these things you have mentioned are indeed going on around me at the moment, but I bet you will not be able to tell me what I do in my other job."

I just laughed and said, "I tell you what, we'll continue with this and at the end we will see if I get it right. I only reveal what the angels and guides show me, I never make things up to make it seem more dramatic, I have to speak the truth, always." While I was saying this to him all I could see floating around him where black wheels. I thought does he sell tires? Does he fix wheels? Is he a mechanic? I was praying for the angels to give me clearer information. I decided to leave it until we had finished. His time with me had ended and he had been given some very good and helpful insight about his situation. He was much happier than when he had arrived and had really enjoyed his visit. Now to his question about his other job, I said, "Pat I have no idea. The only thing I have to say is that during the whole time you sat there all I could see around you were wheels. There were loads of them. Do you work with tyres, sell wheels in a garage or what?"

He started to laugh so much that I did as well. Between laughing and trying to speak he said, "Pauline that is the best I have ever heard! My other job is that I fix the wheels on the wheelie bins for the council."

It made me laugh even more. I would never have guessed that in a million years that was what all the wheels floating around him meant. The angels always show a great sense of humour when showing me answers to particular things.

It was a fun to start working in my beautiful new reading room. I still needed certain bits to finish the room but it would all fall into place. Monte had been busy with work since going back to America and was also studying with the local priest there. It was something he had been doing for a year or two. Religion hadn't been a prerequisite of our relationship, nor was it even posted in our profiles on the dating site where we met. Monte's interest in Catholicism had developed just before we began seeing each other. It was a strange coincidence that some of the people around Monte found hard to believe, but as is so often the case, the truth is stranger than fiction. I didn't get involved in Monte's religious pursuits as I believe that it is something gentle and beautiful when it is let alone to bloom in its own time. After all, it was Monte's journey with God and the Holy Spirit, not mine.

I went off with mum one day to look for the new room furniture. I had a small amount of money set aside, but I really wanted a set of comfortable chairs for my guests. I always include the angels and guides to help me find what I need and this day was no exception. I had no idea of colour or other particulars, just that I would know it when I saw it. We drove around for a while when we came across a place with a sale on. I walked in the door and there it was! But whether I could afford it was another question. Unfortunately the guy I needed to talk to was not there and I had to call back another day. As I was leaving the mill, I just knew I was going to have these chairs for the room. We called in again the next day and I got to chat to the owner. Which turned out even better than I thought it was going to be. The two chairs were on sale and the footstool was added to the package. I got both chairs for the exact amount I had wanted to spend. They were perfect! When I got them delivered it made the room look like you were sitting in a garden outside. The chairs suited the style of the cabin and all the wood made it so cozy. I knew the angels and guides would help and they had. I needed a table and it was the same thing again; I got the perfect table for much less than I thought it would be.

The room was now ready for me to get started. I had everything I needed, but, just like stage fright, doubt crept in. I knew this was where I was going on my path, but I also knew what a big responsibility it is to guide and to help another person in truth and goodness. I was sure that I was being given lots of help through my guides and angels and have really had only to trust and learn the way in which they guide me and not let worry smother the light that was trying to grow. It was like the story of the mother that was so worried about her daughter that she not only prevented her daughter from healing, she neglected to care for herself.

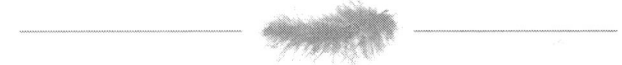

When Lily came to me I knew when she sat down she wanted to know about her health. Lily was a lovely, gentle woman with a family and a wonderful husband, but she had just been diagnosed with cancer. She also had a daughter that suffered from an eating disorder. I could relate to the daughter's situation having gone through it myself. Lily was more worried about her daughter than herself and it was so clear in her time spent with me. When the angels and guides came through, the message was that she also needed to look after herself and that it was not being selfish but was indeed vital. When she gave herself time to be stress free and relax more, she would be able to help her family and her daughter more. The angel's messages told her that things would improve and that she should live her life and let go of the cloud of worry she had over her daughter. This cloud was making the daughter more ill. It is a little like putting your child into a bubble of motherly concern but added in is the mothers worries along with your child's fears and worries, and by doing it you have suffocated your child's right to live and grow.

Lily had to start to let go of the thoughts and the emotions that made her think she was in control of all situations around her. As a mother she can protect, guide and love her daughter but her daughter also has her life path and needs to be able to walk freely to be allowed to bloom in her own way. This blocking, smothering energy had to be released to let everything start to flow again. Six months after Lily's first visit she brought her husband along the next time I got to see her. I was so happy that her husband thought a visit would help him as well. Her health and the worries about her daughter had improved in a wonderful way. Her daughter was being more outgoing and happier than she had been for a long time. It was a gift to me to see Lily again and to know that the angels had helped her drop the worry and lift her energy to start positive growth and health in her family and herself. Lily was still in the middle of her treatment for cancer, but she said she was so positive and felt so well. She did not want to waste a day on thinking of being ill, she only wanted to be able to do as much as she could in a joyful and fulfilled way. Seeing the blessings in her life in that moment, more than the worries of the future, was creating a new state of bliss and happiness and the energy of light and love and powerful healing within her and her family.

What was present in my life at this time was so wonderful. Monte had successfully gone through all the years of study and was now going to be baptised. He was back in Northern Ireland again and was going to be baptised in one of our local chapels. I had never experienced an adult baptism before and it was such a special occasion. The fact that it was Monte made it so much more amazing. We had to arrange Godparents for Monte. It ended up such a laugh, because he got me as his Godmother, and my brother Brendan as his Godfather. His baptism was taking place at Easter, which is a beautiful time for the birth of a new way of being and renewal in our lives. The baptism was a wonderful event when it happened, and we had a great celebration on that Easter Saturday night afterwards. My family members where all present to witness this amazing blessed gathering. It is really special having the lovely gift of a supportive family for occasions like this. It is truly what is important in our lives. The love that we create within that family unit expands outward and is then shared with the outside world.

I had finished my room to get on with my spiritual work. It had taken a while for all the ideas and inspirations for that space to manifest into reality, but now it was all ready to go. Still, I had so many things going on and things I worried about at times. I would always talk to the angels when I would go to bed. I was lying there in bed, my mind spinning with a myriad of things when suddenly the room was filled with golden light. Archangel Michael was there, smiling at me. He was so young and powerful! It only lasted for a few seconds and then it ended. The room was filled with a peacefulness and I fell asleep right away, all my worries washed away. It was the second time I had got to see a vision of Archangel Michael and I know he is always there to call on when I am feeling more fear than hope.

Monte wanted to be spending more time in Northern Ireland than he had before so that was taking place as well. I was trying to keep moving ahead and I was still trying to make a good living. The photography had been so slow to take off that I had really gone completely off the idea of making a go of it. All it had done was eat away at any money I had put into it. I would still get odd jobs to do but my interest was much more focused on my spiritual work. It was what I was passionate about and what engaged my heart and soul. So I set aside the professional photography though I would still go out though and take landscape photography just for relaxation and to clear my mind. It worked wonderfully well to help me with my psychic work for getting rid of any built up of heavy energies. Nature has the most healing light in the world we should try and get outside every day if possible.

Mary came to me because her friend was coming for a reading. Sometimes I can have two friends come to me and the information I receive will end up more important for the friend than the person that booked in the first place. Mary was a counsellor to the bereaved and was always really busy. She was a very strong person and had come through a lot in her own life that made her very qualified to do her job. Her questions were more general and entered around if she was going to get her house sold and move to a new area. When my Guardian angel Serena came through, the guidance was that she would sell her house but to have patience it would take a little bit of time. Serena also brought Mary's father in from the spirit realm and let her feel the tingling energy to let her know he was there. I was shown different things to let Mary know that her father does visit with her from time to time. I was shown a kitchen area in Mary's home and a mug that her father always got his tea in when he would visit Mary when he was alive. This was a great comfort to her and she told me that she had always been aware that she had a person that guided and had helped her in her life from the spirit realm. Mary said that she would have been much more open and had her own experiences of spirit when she was younger but had not thought much about it all until now later in her life. It was when Mary was explaining this to me that the angels then brought two young people from spirit into the room. I could see them but I knew these two young people could not see me at all they where both looking attentively at Mary. I explained to Mary that two more deceased people had arrived a young man called Steven and a younger girl called Laura and that they where standing like they where in a queue to see her. At first she could not understand why they where there, but I was given a very strong message for her that they were to do with her work or connected to someone at her work.

She suddenly put her hand up to her mouth and said, "I am counselling a couple that have just lost a son through suicide and another couple whose young daughter had died suddenly".

As Mary was explaining this to me I could see both the spirit children start to smile. It was so beautiful to watch. I said to Mary, "That is exactly why they are here, your connection to the spirit realm is going to open up again and be used so much more in your work. You will have lots of messages for the people that have lost loved ones." She was a little shocked but also said she felt a wonderful surge of knowing that what she was being told was so true for her. She had come to me thinking of moving home but I think her heart had been moved in the process of the reading. Mary is still working hard and gives powerful comfort to the people that she helps in their loss.

Having a spiritual connection can work through so many jobs that people do it can be an eye opener. Only for my guardian angel and guides I would not be doing the work that I am doing, and it is great to realise that God's angels and guides can work through anyone in any field of work if you invite them in to help. They are the source of all my guidance and help to guide the people that come to me. It can be as overwhelming for me at times as it is for the wonderful people that come my way. Writing about Mary's story can remind all of us that we can do many things in our lives to make a living, but it is what we are called to do that never leaves us. We will always feel a pull or an unease in our life to change if we are not in the right job or any other thing in our lives that is not the correct path. Mary in her youth had a wonderful connection to spirit and had closed that connection due to the ups and downs she had experienced and the pathways she had walked down that had pulled her away from her true calling. But when her life had settled and she found her calling to be a counsellor to the bereaved, her gift was now opening up for her again. The smiles I had seen that day from those two young spirit children was a beautiful affirmation to me and to Mary how much we are needed to help the spiritual realm. We can all go wandering off our true path as I had into photography. I still enjoy it, but it is not what I truly needed to be doing. It is a hobby now and it takes me into nature which is great for my healing and in turn empowers me to be able to help others in my spiritual work.

I have also had people that come to me that have gone off on all kinds of wrong paths because they do not want to hear any kind of loving advice or sound direction. These are people that are only wanting to hear what matches their thoughts or ideas. They are not open to help in their lives or interested in bettering the lives of the people around them. It can be hard to be told you are being selfish or negative and that it needs to be looked at and changed. These people are already in turmoil with themselves and the fight that is going on internally can be really tough to shake off. They want to be confrontational with everything and everyone, but really they need nurturing, understanding and love. It is really the light and the dark within a person that is engaged in battle.

Elaine arrived at my door and wanted to bring in her nephew to sit in while we were talking. I was a little taken back about her wanting to include this fifteen year old boy while she was in with me. I had to tell her that I could not allow her nephew to sit in I made it clear that I take one person at a time. She told me she had taken him to other people and it had been completely fine that he had been there. I still stuck to how I feel about teenagers needing to be eighteen before I will allow them in. Elaine agreed then that, that was fine and I got started to get some advice for her. I always ask people to try and be relaxed and be totally open to get the best healing and information to help them. I also make it clear that what is being given in guidance has nothing to do with me I am just the voice used for God's angels and guides to help them. As we got started, the information I was relaying to Elaine was clear and concise. I continued on and as I got to a part that included family arguments and confrontations Elaine completely shut down. I saw her shiver openly when I mentioned this. I knew this was crucial issue for her because after this, the same issues kept coming out no matter how long we carried on. I eventually said to her I had to stop because I was not getting anything new, her angels and guides were staying on the same subject. Elaine was quick to reply to me that she did not know of any family issues and that she was really disappointed that first her nephew had not been allowed in and secondly that I had stopped. I could see her anger and frustration towards me, but I can only relay with what is shown to me. If it stays on one subject and the person the information is for is in denial, then the help is falling on deaf ears. To most people they see only me, but it is so much more than that. I have to work within truth and integrity to my angels and guides of God's love. I am just the voice to speak up and not allow people to forget that the angels are also present and it is such an honour that they are there to help them. I knew what Elaine had been shown was correct and true about her family issues and there was a lot of anger present around her at this time. She left and I asked her to remember to ask the angels for help in her life. I do know that Elaine did take on board what had been said to her and that the problems remain that way if they are not looked at and resolved. It was made very clear from her reading that everything would stay the same if she did not deal with, and really look at what was presently going on around her in her life and her attitude in thinking that she was completely in the right to be angry and aggressive. There can be no healing in anger and fear, only pain will remain that needs to be healed.

Ruth came to me because as she said she wanted change in her life. In a similar way to Elaine she did not want to hear what needed to be done for the changes to happen. Ruth wanted to sit back and see things move forward but when Serena, Mat and John let her know that she had to move and change in certain ways for things to get better she got more annoyed. Ruth blamed everyone else in her life for her situation. She blamed her husband, her family, her work colleagues and so on. No matter what she was shown or what I was guided to say to her she stayed in the past or on a negative present happening. I did think that at least she wanted change so maybe that was a good start. The message stayed on the same topics; quarrels, arguments and stagnant issues. I told Ruth that she had to look at how she was reacting to the people that loved her in her life and if she could find it in her heart to first of all forgive herself and be gentle with her loved ones that would make a strong wonderful change. She was guided to see that people were just being a mirror to her, showing her how her behaviour was creating the worries and dramas surrounding her. Her negative outlook and energy had to be shifted and love is the only answer to help that. Love for herself first and then love for others around her. It may take some time but I know Ruth has an inner beauty that she will find by releasing her need to be in control of everything and everyone around her. Ruth had closed down in the visit to me because she was not hearing what she wanted to hear. God's angels and guides are not here to appease our whims, they don't always give us what we want but they do give us what we need for the good of all. Ruth left that day saying she was disappointed, but I know she also left with the messages she had received to help her. I pray that Ruth and Elaine are doing much better and have found how powerful a loving heart and a gentle nature can be. The angels of God's light will always help but they have to be invited into people lives to do so, I always ask and hope that people leave me with a realisation of how amazing that gift is to all of us on earth.

Pauline Johnson

CHAPTER 21

A Heavenly Gift

As I write this, I realise how much God's angels and guides have accompanied me throughout my life. Even when I have closed down to their help and gone off in a wrong direction they never left me. It's a wonderful thing that our angels and spirit guides are here for all of us and never leave us. Every one of us on earth has Heavenly gifts that surround us every day. The most beautiful of these is God's love. We don't have to look for His love, it is within us and surrounds us always. More sharing of this love could change things here on earth in a tremendous way for the better. Every single person on earth has been given this incredible heavenly friend and companion our guardian angel. They bring such beauty and amazing guidance in your life. I have seen this over and over in my own life and in the lives of others. The power of this wonderful gift never ceases to amaze me. Serena is present with me at every tick of the clock, day and night. It is Serena that introduced the other guides and angels into my life and brings through the deceased in a protected way. When we truly acknowledge the two beautiful divine aspects of God's love and our guardian angel's love for us, it will change how we see each other and help us know how much divine help we have.

You are never alone. Quite the opposite, you are guided and protected if you allow yourself to be. The beautiful fact is that God's love is the most real love; filled with mercy, patience, peace, contentment and joy. I talk to my guardian angel Serena every day and it has only strengthened my ability to know when she needs me to be still and listen. It is with your own trust and faith you will be able to hear your guardian angel.

A Heavenly Gift

People always ask me what their angel looks like. The amazing thing is, just as we are all unique and individual so are the angels. Serena is female in appearance to me, so beautiful with a brilliant white light that surrounds her. The light is so dazzling that prevents me from seeing any details to the point where I can't even answer the question as to whether or not she has wings. I think that anyone who gets to see their own guardian angel will see them in whatever way is the most comfortable for them. You can get acquainted with your guardian angel simply by beginning to realise that they are with you. Try this right now: think of this divine gift. The gift that gives you your very own guardian angel. They have been with you even before you were born; there to guide and love you like no-one on this earth can. Your angel will never doubt in you, never judge you and never leave you, no matter what happens in your life. Invite your angel to draw closer to you, just ask with a smile and say hello!

We all have the gift of communication with God. It's one of His gifts to us. We don't have to be in a certain place to connect to God. We are all His children and we are never apart from Him. Prayer of course is what comes to mind when I think of communication with Our Lord and believe me, prayer makes a huge difference. I have been shown this when praying for the souls in purgatory. They may have only requested one prayer but that one prayer creates a transformation that is breathtaking. I will try to tell you what I see when I have been requested to pray for a soul in purgatory. I can't see much of where they are, just the souls themselves. These poor souls have a dull shimmering, shifting grey light about them, their grey robes hang loosely. They have an expression on their face like they are in crippling pain. Their eyes seem to be pleading for help. My feeling is that there is an urgency to pray for them. The prayers that they need are told to me, how many they need and it is always different for each soul. The prayers have to be heart felt and focused and the effect is breathtaking. Once the prayers have been said the greyness and anguish disappear from their faces and is replaced with a youthful softness and the most beautiful smile. Their robes are now white and they are surrounded with a glow of brilliant white. They sometimes wave and thank me or just leave, going upwards in such an ecstatic state of grace and joy. It is a moment of pure bliss when this happens.

Prayer from a loving, faith filled heart can change any situation and is the best way to find peace of mind and wisdom. It is crucial to my work that I ask for guidance and to be filled with the Holy Spirit to help me with everything in my own life while doing my work. I would like to make one very important point - I do not pray *to* angels. I do ask that they carry my requests. I ask for intercessions and prayers from our Mother Mary and the saints to help me. God hears our requests and will not always give us what we want, but will give us what we truly need. I try to have pure intent in prayer and it can be hard at times. Making prayer an everyday part of your life will bring a greater connection and a deeper relationship to God.

We have all been given this heavenly gift of prayer. Using it often for others and ourselves will send divine healings, blessings and love to everyone. A prayer can be just a few simple words it does not have to be long and drawn out.

My spirit guides are Mat, John, Beth and Bearl and they are a gift that has given me so much joy and invaluable blessed guidance. They help me communicate clearly with the deceased and give me direction while speaking to the people that come to me. I have at times been given the names of other people's spirit guides as well. Asking for your spirit guide to help you will strengthen and deepen the relationship that you have with them. In rare cases spirit guides can be people that you have known that have passed away, but in my experience they are usually complete strangers that have come from heaven to help us here.

Guides have to be qualified, in a manner of speaking, before they can interact with us. They are evolved and enlightened though still very much individuals with their own personalities and mannerisms. They are not given to us to agree or disagree with our choices, they are here to guide us and purify our intentions. I know which of my guides are with me from the feeling I get on each side of my body. One way to tell if the guidance you get is correct is that it should always be positive kind and loving. If it is negative in any way, ask Archangel Michael to step in and clear the energy. Also remember the name of Jesus said three times will get rid of anything that is spiritually negative. A bad spirit cannot stay around when Our Lord's name is used in this way. It is the most powerful protection.

Of course it's easy to forget that one of the most wonderful gifts we have been given is that of free will. Our right to choose our own fate is at the very core of creation itself. It is amazing to me though how often people refuse to accept responsibility for their choices. We are all here to learn lessons and to improve as people and to love and care more for others when we have gone through difficult times. Certainly we all make bad choices, give in to temptation and even wander off down dangerous paths. When we find ourselves somewhere we don't want to be that is usually when we call out for help. Taking responsibility for our part in the trouble we face is one of the best ways to invite help from your angels and guides. There is an old saying that goes 'Let go and let God.' When you really think about it, it makes perfect sense. Our Heavenly Father will always welcome back even the most wayward of people. God stands with open arms not wanting anyone to feel guilty or unworthy of His mercy and love. We cannot be presumptuous of His mercy, thinking that we can do what we like and we will always be forgiven. In our free will, asking God to forgive us from a humble heart with true intent brings the miracle of His love and protection back into our lives.

As this chapter is all about gifts, I would be remiss if I didn't talk about the gift of continuance, that is to say; life after death. Death is an existence just like life, I have experienced this first hand and have been witness to many deceased family and friends coming through to help and heal their loved ones on earth. When I do a reading my first priority is to get out of the way and make sure I am centred and grounded for any communication that may come through. It is such an amazing experience each time a deceased person comes through and the angels bring messages. The experience of this blessed communication is just one of the wonderful benefits of doing God's work here. Heavenly energy is thrilling, eye opening and immensely peaceful. A guardian angel can come through in a form of beautiful sparkles of light or I will be shown images of them with a person's deceased loved ones as they walk toward us. The angels are dressed in the most beautiful coloured robes. They are regal and always beautiful. Their light is immense and it has a wing shape to it that surrounds them. They talk to me in the way a human being would. It can be very humorous at times and other times quite serious. I get to see the orbs of light dancing gently around the people that come to me. It is lovely to watch and to feel this amazing energy of love and affection that their angel has for them. I always tell people that they will feel much lighter and more relaxed during and after the reading. The reason for this is that the angels are moving around them while they sit and are literally cleansing the aura during the reading. The affect of this makes a huge difference for the person being read. Worries are lifted and a new feeling of hope returns. I get to see it in their eyes and faces. Of course it also depends on how open the person is to healing and moving forward in their lives, letting go of the past and accepting change. You have free will and the angels never interfere with that. You have to want help, invite them into your life to help you step forward into a new way of being as well as take the steps to make the necessary changes in your life. Asking them for help always creates a positive influence.

When the angels bring a deceased family member or friend in during a reading a wonderful warm tingling feeling usually accompanies them. Sometimes the person being read gets to feel this beautiful energy as well, it can be very up lifting. All the deceased people that come through are coming from Heaven and are protected and surrounded by the guardian angels and guides that help them interact. I never call or ask for anyone from the spirit realm to be with us. The reason for this is that thinking in our human way that we have the control or possibility to do this without protection from God and the angels brings in the wrong energy. Calling spirits or requesting them to be present can present an opportunity for dark, negative, or dangerous entities to also come through. Trust me, that is not something you ever want to deal with. People use all kinds of things to summon the deceased. Things like a ouija board can look like a bit of fun, but it can have some very bad outcomes that are not easy to rectify. It is up to God and my guardian angel Serena to pick and choose who is to come through for each person. Not everyone that comes in for a reading will have a deceased family member or friend come through. Sometimes it is more important to receive the messages that are given from the angels.

My guides let me know about the issues that need to be talked about. They also communicate to me in the form of mental images. For example, when the deceased are present they can show me inside the clients home or work and even to items. They can show me what the client may have been doing earlier that day or week, especially if it pertains to the deceased person's connection with the one being read. A particular item in their home can be pertinent to the person being read for. Each reading is unique for each individual. Sometimes it can be difficult for me to put all the pieces together to make sense of the messages. I am shown fleeting images that come so quickly I have to be really grounded to catch the detail. I have to pick up on the feelings I am sensing, the words I am hearing, the images I see and the knowing that goes along with all of these things. I am never sure what my wonderful heavenly friends have in store for me. I am just their helper and I am so grateful to be able to do what I do.

I'd like to focus for a minute on continuance; the fact that we live on after our bodies die, because it is very real and such a gift. It is so important to the people left behind to know that their loved ones are in a beautiful place and looked after so lovingly. I have been permitted to see visions of the angels working with deceased family members in beautiful gardens while doing a reading. There are trillions of these gardens, each one unique for each family. Flowers are planted and weeds taken out to represent gifts that are on the way to a family or things that have come to an end. Our deceased family pray for us with the angels to protect us and watch over us. When the grannies, granddads, mothers, fathers, brothers, sisters, children and friends come through they are happy, beaming with colour and light. The feeling that comes with them is tremendous love for us on earth. They come through to give us their acquired Heavenly strength that touches the people sitting with me in an amazing way. They bring back to us what we feel we have lost or are weak in. Things like faith, belief, hope, joy, peace, trust, and love both for ourselves and towards others. Always remember the gift of continuance. You are eternal and the ones who have passed on are always very close by.

While we're on the subject of gifts I would be truly remiss not to talk about the gift of providence. The word itself is often misunderstood and I had to look it up to make sure I had the complete meaning. According to my dictionary it simply means: The protective care of God or of nature as a spiritual power. Examples of providence surround us constantly in our everyday lives. Being out in nature and getting to experience the vastness of creation, whether it's on television or we get to visit in person, is incredible. The uplifting beauty of the oceans, forests, mountains and deserts can have a fabulous healing effect for all of us. God sustains all things, plans all things and is everywhere for us at all times even if we are not consciously aware of it. The way the seasons appear is according to perfect divine timing and we are no different. Always remember that everything falls into place in His time. Spring is a great time to just sit and listen to nature coming alive. Just as nature is renewed over and over continually so it is in our lives. Things will happen when they are meant to. If we push or try to control the outcome it only brings frustration and discontentment to us.

As you meditate on nature turn your attention inward to the wonderful creation that is us. Think of the detail He has put into each human being. We could say that our essence is like a diamond. Each of us is born with a beautiful shining soul; unique and incredibly detailed. Some facets shine brightly while others have yet to be polished. That is what we are here to do - polish as many of the facets of ourselves so we can shine brighter to help light each other's way. The more we take time and work on what needs polishing up in our own lives, the better. From the least detail to the most important, involve your angels and guides and Heaven will plan the very best outcome for you. Things will fall into place in the most amazing ways when you address your requests to God.

A Heavenly Gift

God is love and so much more. He has given us everything we could ever need including the most precious gift in the ability to love. In addition to this, by giving us free will, God has given us the choice to love Him and each other. This does not mean that you should love to your detriment or to anyone else's either. It means that you should love in a true, honest, pure way. Love your husband, wife, or partner, love your pets, love your family, love your friends, love yourself and of course love God. Let others know that you love them, and not just through your words. Love must also show through in your actions. Words said with no loving actions are empty and pointless. Ask your angels to bring love into your life through all your relationships and start to see a blessed change. When we are done on this earth it will not matter how much money you had, what job you did here, how many houses you owned, or if your car is the latest model. We cannot take any of these things with us when we leave here. These things are an illusion. We do of course have to be responsible and have enough to pay our bills, that's part of living but, we came with nothing and we leave with nothing. When our soul goes back home to Heaven I think the most important question we will be asked is, how did we love others while being here on earth? Or maybe, do we think we loved enough?

One of the delightful experiences I have been given was to see a vision of the person that another will fall in love with. The first time it happened I was looking at this beautiful girl sitting in front of me. While she was speaking to me I could see a male standing behind her smiling. Even more shocking was that the male was one of my brothers! I could see him clearly but he would appear and then disappear. At the time the two had yet to meet and the appearance of an apparition of my brother, who is very much alive, completely baffled me. I should have trusted what Serena was showing me because sure enough, without any intervention from me, the two managed to meet, fall in love, get married and now have three beautiful children. I am so happy for them, they are an amazing couple.

I thought this was a one-off because of the family connection, but this was only the beginning. The second time it happened I had gone into a local shop. The girl at the counter patiently tried to help me but all I could do was stare." I could see the face of a guy I knew that owned a bar in another town close to her. I left that day really wanting to say something to her but didn't. She must have thought I was nuts! The next time I went into the shop, I remember it was raining hard and my shoes squeaked on the floor. Thankfully she was working alone behind the counter. "Serena" I thought, "I hope you are right about this." I swallowed hard and said, "Hi, I don't now if you remember me from the other day, I wonder do you ever go to Monaghan to any of the bars there." I mentioned a particular bar to her and if she knew the owner.

She answered, "I know the place, but not the guy."

"The next time you go in there," I said, "say hello to John, he owns the bar."

She laughed and took it quite well really as she did not know who I was. Seven years later I was sitting in my hair dresser's salon relaying this story to her and saying I would have loved to know the outcome, when she said, "I know the girl you are talking about, she comes in here to get her hair done!" She had gone to the bar and was now married to John and they had just had their first baby. Indeed it is very rare when I know the reasons why I am compelled to give the information that I give. I am simply the go-between, 'the messenger' if you will. From that moment on, the next time I was shown to tell someone about love in their lives I wouldn't hesitate to speak up.

Please know that each day God's angels are here ready to help you with everything. From the birth of a child to the loss of a loved one, they want to be involved in your daily lives and stand waiting to be invited. Angels attract to you when you call on them, but it must be for the greatest good. Angels vibrate at the highest level and they cannot help if the intentions of a person are for their own greed, jealousy, or harm to another person. A request or intention from a loving heart is enough. It is always wonderful when I get to witness the energy and light around the angels. They resonate to different colours and different types of music and can use these ways to communicate to us here on earth. But they are not the only ones who shine. I see colours and light shining around people as well. Oddly, the best way I can come up with to describe the colours is to use the words like 'childlike' and 'playful'. The angels colours are vivid, gold, purple, electric blue, green, white; the angels are really the rainbow in our everyday clouds. I am not special, anyone can learn to see these things. Just try being still for a little while each day, relax your mind and listen. To connect to your own guardian angel it's best to start with an invitation. Don't expect immediate results, but with regular practice you will begin to see more clearly. Remember keep your heart open, connect with nature every day if possible, play soft music, read about the angels, ask for a sign from them. White feathers may start to appear around you, pennies or butterflies. Your angel knows you better than anyone so they may leave you signs that mean something particularly important to you. You don't get a say in what the signs will be, just be open in heart, mind and spirit. You may start to hear more songs with the word 'angels' in it, or see other signs in nature. That is the angels letting you know you are connected to them. Trust the warm peaceful feeling you get as well when you think of your guardian angel, that is your angel giving you a loving hug. Your guardian angel is responsible for letting your spirit guides into your life and bringing the deceased forward with messages. They are a bit like the door keeper that keeps you safe and protected while connecting in a spiritual way.

Earlier I wrote about some of my life growing up and how as children we are innocent, light and open to other people. It is such pity as we get into adulthood some of us begin to close down. We can become filled with guilt and our light dims because we choose to hold on to hurts, and that can leave us in a very skeptical frame of mind, shutting out the world and sealing us away from the light and love we so desperately need. Sometimes we have suffered at the hands of others, whether through words or actions. We all have the choice as to how we react to the mishaps in our lives. But mostly we react quickly, without much thought. This is where the examples that Our Lord gave us through His life can be used to show us that we can shine through it all. Always ask your own guides and your guardian angel to help you when negative situations arise. When you involve God it brings the most powerful love and positive change to any situation. Being childlike and letting go to let God take over is not easy as an adult, but it is truly all that is needed. We are all God's children and that is why the angels and guides are there to direct us and give us their divine help. We have been given so many gifts. When we realise this completely within our hearts the power of His words, "Peace I leave with you, my peace I give you." will truly be felt.

Becoming aware of the presence of the deceased in my life helped me to have compassion for anyone who has lost a loved one. The intense emotions and the emptiness we are left with can be completely overwhelming. Our loved ones have gone with the angels to a beautiful place and we are left behind, missing them every day. Seeing the effect on a person's health and mental state after a death is so hard to watch. There does not seem to be any comfort no matter what direction you turn. When my father passed I distracted myself from the pain with material things and wanted to be on the go constantly, when really I should have been looking inward for peace and love. But I was also only thirteen years old so looking inward was the last place I wanted to go. I learned the lesson the hard way - you cannot run from yourself. Buried grief and anger manifests itself eventually in other ways. I kept the tears in check and didn't deal with how I was feeling inside. For some it is all too easy in those circumstances to drink too much, or take drugs or use other outward means to ease the pain, but it only makes a bad situation worse. Alcohol and drugs dim our very being and we go to the darker side of our nature. The angels call alcohol 'poison', and remind us to not drink poison with weak minded people.

There is no avoiding the truth, and the truth is that pain has to be dealt with eventually. This is another place where prayer is so powerful. I prayed as a child when I lost my own father and I know the strength we all felt at his funeral. It was not our own strength, it came from God. We even talked about it when we came home that day about how calm we all felt. For me it was like watching someone else's funeral, not my own dad's. I do know we where given help to get through the day, but the pain of loss can take years to come to terms with. We have to be so gentle with ourselves to start the healing process.

I still pray about everything in my life. I pray that I am getting the correct guidance and help while doing my work, that I will have good health, that the day will be wonderful, the list is endless. I say the rosary, it can be prayer in short form in your own words or it can be said in other prayers you know. It does not have to be perfect, just thinking this way will bring your angels and guides to your side without fail. I open myself up and invite them in to the problem or situation and thank them for being with me. I try my best to remind myself that I am just the person being used to help and that it is God's angels that are there with their amazing healing energy and wisdom.

Lessons in Grounding, Centring & Meditation

I would like to take a minute to talk about the importance of being grounded. It's an actual exercise that I do and find it very valuable and rewarding. To give this gift to yourself, take some quiet time for yourself and find a comfortable, calm place to be. I usually ground myself by standing. I visualise roots growing down from my feet into the ground. I try to make them as deep into the strong earth as I can possibly imagine. Once the roots are anchored, I picture them growing back up over my feet and up my ankles. Usually when I do this I feel a slight tug, this lets me know I am now grounded, firmly rooted to the full weight of the earth.

Next, I centre myself. This is another important aspect of being ready to receive clear information. I take a deep breath and visualise a white light coming down through the top of my head, filling my entire body all the way down to my feet. Being centred is being focused within your own being to your heart and feeling balanced.

I also suggest meditation. Meditation can be different for everyone but it will take you out of your mind and turn off the worldly noise for a while. Over time this will strengthen your psychic and intuitive abilities. As always, invite your heavenly friends in to help you do this. I find that being out in nature really helps me get into the meditative state but when I can't, I try to pick a time and place where I can find the most quiet. Meditation is finding the still, silent peace within and listening to the world as it happens around you. As you breath in and out, try to pay attention as you are become more relaxed and as your breath slows and deepens. Feel your breath moving in and out like a wave on the beach slowly and gently lapping the shore. You can choose how long you want to do this exercise.

If that doesn't work for you then there is the colour technique. What you do is focus on a colour that feels right to you. Visualise this colour in your mind, if you see it fade bring it back to your attention. Try to hold it for as long as you can. Start with holding it in your minds eye for a count of ten. Repeat this two more times. Over time you will be able to increase the amount of time you can hold the colour in your mind. This will not only strengthen your ability to focus but give you a feeling of peace and calm that can affect your whole day. Connecting with spirit happens in different ways for everyone. I can only tell you what I do.

I always start with a prayer for connection, guidance and protection. I always ask God to send me help in the name of Jesus. That help then comes through my guardian angel Serena and my guides Mat and John. I ask for the most blessed guidance for all concerned. It is important for me personally that I feel the source of guidance connecting to me through my heart because, when I wish to give messages or help, I need to do it with love, wisdom and compassion. Take time to notice the feeling of connecting, of being cared for and of being open to wisdom and love. By regularly practising these exercises you will notice a real change in your ability to connect with your angels and guides. Meditation to help silence the mind, grounding that helps us to be realistic and authentic about the angels and guides being in our lives, getting centred to be balanced and internally strong to help us feel and know when guidance is right and appropriate or what is not right for us. Then being connected in all these ways helps us receive the wisdom and love from Heaven. These are some of the steps I take to help with what I do. I hope they will be helpful to you as well.

Lifestyle does play an important part in helping me help others. It can be exhausting to do this work, but certain things can really help. Being healthy and getting lots of rest is a wonderful start. I eat lightly before I see someone for their appointment but for some reason I always feel the need to eat something sweet afterwards. I have no idea why I crave sweet things, it's just that way for me. To ease the craving I try to have some fruit instead of sweets. I also wash my hands afterwards. Good old soap and warm water is grounding and helps me start to come down from the high vibration that I have been in while doing a reading. Getting out for a bit of a walk afterwards is good as well. Nature and exercise moves and clears the energy. It is really important for me to be grounded after meeting with a person, but it is equally important for me to clear myself as well. I cannot hold on to any of the words or emotions of the person I have just met with, if I did I would make myself very ill. This is one of the down sides of being empathic. Always pray that your energy is protected, but when you feel your own emotions start to get carried away by other's it's vital to draw your energy back. Empaths have a tendency to reach out to others. It's important to know the difference between sympathy and empathy. Both are vital in the way we treat each other in this world but for someone with an empathic gift it can be difficult to stay emotionally grounded. Pray, do the exercises and be mindful is the best advice I can give. In the end, your emotions are you own and your are responsible for controlling them.

    Now, let's talk about where you are doing your work. Whether it's on for yourself or if you are embarking on doing this work it is important to clear the space. Both before and afterwards. Playing gentle music and keeping the space where you work filled with only beautiful things helps to keep the vibrations at a higher level. Being positive and asking for Heavenly assistance is always the best option for me and as always, practice mindfulness, pray, ground and centre.

I am so humbled by the people that come my way. They can have all kinds of things going on but I find that most people are trying their best no matter how bad life is. I have seen such strength in people. These people have been a true inspiration to me in my own life. They give me strength and courage to do more with my life and not wallow in things that are not important. It has made me wonder at times if I could be that strong if I was in their position.

There is one constant message that comes from Heaven; to be gentle with each other, have hope, let love into your heart, let go of hate, be less judgmental and try to forgive. We all have a long way to go and it is comforting to know we all have incredible help to clear away the sorrow and worries that we all go through on our journey here on earth.

Pauline Johnson

Conclusion

Thank you for joining me on this journey, for taking the time to read this little book. The last thing I want to add is the single most important thing that helps me do this work, and that is faith. I stumbled on a saying that I really like. It goes, "You don't worship religion, you worship God." Practicing this keeps me on the right path. I go to Mass each week and I pray and talk to God and His angels every day as well the guides that have been sent my way to help me and others. I love to see people coming my way. They are not here by chance, they have been brought to me. There are a lot of good healers, psychic and mediums in this world, but there are also a lot of people that are working under false pretences. It is always a good idea to check out as much as you can about the medium, psychic or healer you go to see. Pray for the guidance and protection that you will be led to the right person to help you. I always say this particular prayer before I meet with a person to do my work. It is a prayer that comes from St Francis of Assisi.

> *Great God, full of glory, and*
> *Thou my Lord Jesus Christ!*
> *I entreat you to enlighten me*
> *And to dispel the darkness of my mind,*
> *To give me a pure faith, a firm hope*
> *and an ardent charity.*
> *Let me have a perfect knowledge of thee,*
> *O God! So that I may in all things be guided by thy*
> *Light, and act in conformity to Thy will.*

A Heavenly Gift

This beautiful prayer is so important to me. Despite the mistrust I have met from skeptics and naysayers I cannot deny the truth of what I have experienced and so I will continue on this path. The rewards far outweigh the burden of this beautiful gift. I am doing what I am supposed to be doing, with a gift that was given to me to help others. I do my work with a heart filled with love of God and love of others on this earth. To do it any other way would be wrong to me. People will always decide for themselves what to believe. I did not see myself ever writing a book in my life. When I was younger at age six or seven I would see other girls my age with diaries and would always think, *I would not want to write down my thoughts, dreams or secrets for other people to see*! Now I have to laugh at the irony as I finish this last chapter. This is my story and I have been given a very blessed life; in the family I was born into, the love that surrounds me, and incredible job I get to do. I get to help my guardian angel and spirit guides help others on earth and I thank God every day for this. To me it is truly a Heavenly Gift.

Pauline Johnson

Appendices

Prayers & Verses in A Heavenly Gift
[Matthew 16:19]

"I tell you the truth, whatever you bind on earth will be bound in heaven, and whatever you loose on earth will be loosed in heaven."

The Prayer to Saint Michael

Saint Michael the Archangel, defend us in battle.
Be our protection against the wickedness
And snares of the devil.
May God rebuke him, we humbly pray;
And do Thou, O Prince of the Heavenly Host-
By the Divine Power of God-
Cast into hell, Satan and all the evil spirits,
Who roam throughout the world
Seeking the ruin of souls.
Amen.

Pauline Johnson

The short prayer for the souls in Purgatory
*"Please God relieve the poor suffering
souls in Purgatory."*

Prayer of St Gertrude the Great
*Eternal Father, I offer thee
the most precious blood
of thy divine son, Jesus
in union with the masses
said throughout the world today
for all the Holy Souls in Purgatory,
for sinners everywhere,
for sinners in the universal Church
and those in my own home and family.*

Guardian Angel Prayer
*Oh Angel of God my Guardian dear,
To whom Gods love commits me here
Ever this day and night,
Be at my side, to light and guard,
To rule and guide, Amen.*

[1 Corinthians 13:4-7]

Love is patient, love is kind.
It does not envy, it does not boast, it is not proud.
It does not dishonour others, it is not self-seeking,
It is not easily angered, it keeps no record of wrong doing.
Love does not delight in evil but rejoices with the truth.
It always protects, always trusts,
Always hopes, always perseveres.
Love never fails.

Prayer of St Francis of Assisi

Great God, full of glory, and
Thou my Lord Jesus Christ!
I entreat you to enlighten me
And to dispel the darkness of my mind,
To give me a pure faith, a firm hope
and an ardent charity.
Let me have a perfect knowledge of thee,
O God! So that I may in all things be guided by thy
Light, and act in conformity to Thy will.

PAULINE JOHNSON

Pauline Johnson has been a professional medium for over fifteen years. She enjoys nature photography, singing, cooking, motorbikes, skiing and generally being outdoors. She is based in Co. Tyrone, Northern Ireland and travels abroad regularly.

To learn more about Pauline's work, book a reading or schedule events please visit:

www.angelwoodhouse.com

www.facebook.com/AngelwoodPauline

Printed in Great Britain
by Amazon